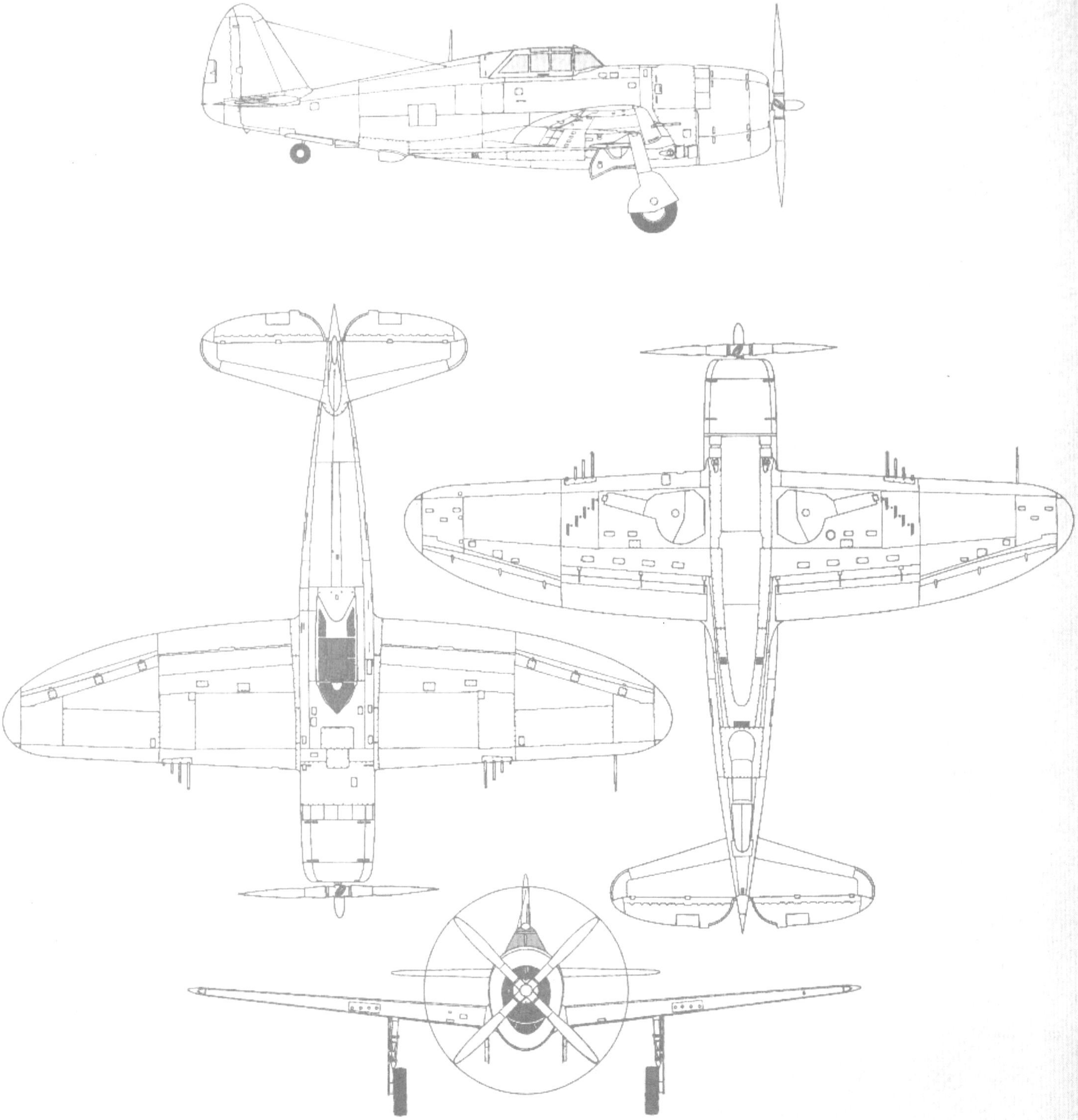

Republic P-47D-11-RE Thunderbolt

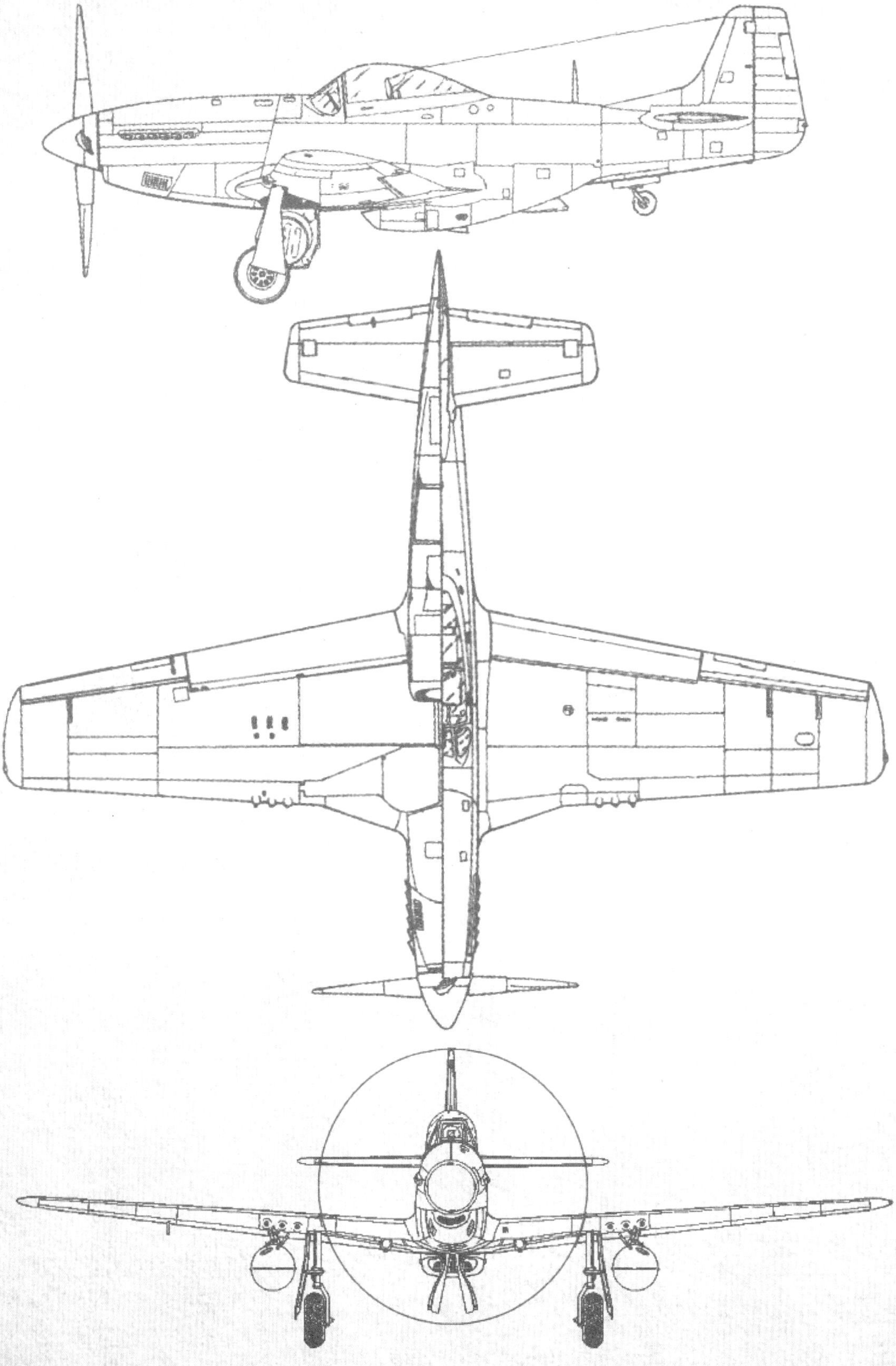

North American P-51D Mustang

JAN LANTMEETERS

COMRADE IN ARMS

The 57 fallen Allied soldiers of the Y-29
De 57 gesneuvelde geallieerde soldaten van de Y-29

In memory of the inauguration
of the memorial for the Blenheim P6912
5-7 July 2024

Thank you!

Colofon
Copyright © 2020: Jan Lantmeeters
www.Y29asch.be

Wettelijk depot D/2021/Jan Lantmeeters, uitgever
ISBN: 9789464070033

Vormgeving: Gordt Lantmeeters
Drukker: Realise Printing

Voorwoord

Van 26 november 1944 tot 27 mei 1945 werd de Advanced Landing Ground (ALG) Y-29 Asch gebruikt door drie Amerikaanse Fighter Groups en één Amerikaanse Bomber Group.

De jachtvliegtuigen en halfzware bommenwerpers werden bemand door jonge piloten met een leeftijd tussen twintig en achtentwintig jaar oud. Deze vaak weinig ervaren piloten werden in de strijd geworpen om doelen aan te vallen en te bombarderen.

Overal was er het gevreesde Duitse afweergeschut dat de vliegtuigen uit de lucht schoot en ook waren de Duitse jachtvliegtuigen van de partij die hun grondgebied hard verdedigden.

Verschillende geallieerde piloten keerden niet meer terug naar de Y-29. Sommigen konden tijdig hun vliegtuig verlaten om met een parachute neer te komen, waarna ze in krijgsgevangenschap eindigden. Anderen hadden minder geluk en stortten neer met hun vliegtuig.

Van de 57 gesneuvelde geallieerde soldaten, verbonden aan Y-29 Asch, kwamen er 27 om nadat hun vliegtuig geraakt werd door afweergeschut (FlaK), 14 stierven tijdens een luchtgevecht, 11 door een crash, 2 bij een bombardement, 2 bij een ongeval en 1 soldaat stierf door een onbekende oorzaak.

Daarbuiten waren er nog verschillende militairen die zwaar gekwetst waren en soms verminkt voor de rest van hun leven.

Deze uitgave wil alle geallieerde soldaten herdenken die hun leven gaven voor de vrijheid van Europa terwijl ze verbonden waren aan Y-29 Asch.

Preface

From November 26th, 1944 to May 27th, 1945 Advanced Landing Ground (ALG) Y-29 Asch was used by three American Fighter Groups and one American Bomber Group.

The fighters and light bombers were manned by young pilots, aged between twenty and twenty-eight years old. These often less experienced pilots were thrown into battle to attack and bomb the assigned targets.

Everywhere there were the dreaded German anti-aircraft guns and German fighters planes who were defending their territory.

Several Allied pilots did not return to the Y-29 Asch. Some were able to bail out in time from their plane with their parachute, but as soon as they landed they were captured. Others were less fortunate and crashed with their planes.

Of the 57 fallen Allied soldiers, attached to Y-29 Asch, 27 died after their plane was hit by anti-aircraft guns (FlaK), 14 died during air combat, 11 crashed, 2 by bombings on the airbase, 2 died in an accident and 1 soldier died from an unknown cause.

There were several other soldiers who were severely injured, some even maimed for the rest of their lives.

This edition will commemorate all Allied soldiers who gave their lives for the freedom of Europe while they were attached to Y-29 Asch.

ALG Y-29 Asch, korte geschiedenis

Half september 1944 werd Zutendaal en omstreken door de geallieerden bevrijd van vier jaar bezetting door de Duitsers. De oorlog was echter nog niet afgelopen. Na de uitbraak uit Normandië waren de geallieerden snel opgerukt maar kwamen tot stilstand aan de grenzen van Duitsland. Het werd snel duidelijk dat de Duitsers hun land hevig zouden verdedigen.

Van 2 tot 21 oktober 1944 was er de slag om Aken en gelijktijdig wilde men ten zuidenoosten van Aken, via het Hürtgenwald, verder Duitsland binnen dringen om zo het industriegebied rond de Roer en daarna de Rijn te bereiken. In dit gebied lag de Siegfriedlinie of Westwall.

De rivier de Roer, stromend door het Hürtgenwald, was voor de geallieerden van groot strategisch belang, vooral de in deze rivier gelegen dammen. De Duitsers konden een groot deel van het Roerdal, tot soms 7,5 meter diep, onder water zetten en zo de geallieerde opmars in Duitsland stoppen.

Om voldoende luchtsteun te krijgen, werd op 3 november 1944 beslist om een vooruitgeschoven vliegveld, Advanced Landing Ground, aan te leggen te Zutendaal. Hierdoor zou de aanvliegtijd van vliegbasis tot vijandelijk doel ingekort worden van één uur naar een kwartier waardoor er meer tijd boven vijandelijk gebied voorhanden was.

Twee dagen later, op 5 november 1944, werd door het 852 Engineer Aviation Battalion begonnen aan de aanleg van de Advanced Landing Ground (ALG) Y-29. Gelegen volledig op het grondgebied van Wiemesmeer (gehucht van Zutendaal), langs de weg van As naar Bilzen, kreeg het de naam van de noordelijk aangrenzende gemeente Asch (nu As).

In amper eenentwintig dagen tijd werd het vliegveld gebouwd, bestaande uit één enkele start- en landingsbaan van 1500 meter die aangelegd werd met PSP platen. Dit waren stalen platen van 3 meter lang en 40 centimeter breed, voorzien van 3 rijen ronde gaten waardoor de sterkte bewaard bleef maar toch licht genoeg was om gemakkelijk mee te werken. Aan de zijkanten waren haken en ogen aangebracht zodat iedere plaat aan elkaar gehaakt kon worden.

Op 26 november 1944 landden de P-47 Thunderbolts jachtvliegtuigen van de 366 Fighter Group op hun nieuwe basis. Nog diezelfde dag werden de eerste missies vanaf Y-29 Asch gevlogen richting Hürtgenwald.

Op 16 december 1944 lanceerden de Duitsers het Ardennenoffensief. Daarmee doofden de gevechten in het Hürtgenwald tijdelijk uit. De missies vanuit Y-29 Asch gingen vanaf dan richting Ardennen. Ter versterking werd op 23 december 1944 de 352 Fighter Group met P-51 Mustangs jachtvliegtuigen vanuit Bodney (Groot-Brittannië) naar Y-29 Asch gestuurd.

Op 1 januari 1945 werd Y-29 Asch aangevallen door tientallen Duitse jagers tijdens de Operation Bodenplatte. Het hierop volgende luchtgevecht zal de geschiedenis ingaan als "The Legend of Y-29", met een groot succes voor de geallieerden.

Na het mislukken van het Ardennenoffensief, het laatste grote Duitse offensief in het westen, hervatten de Amerikanen op 10 januari 1945 de strijd in het Hürtgenwald. Deze slag om het Hürtgenwald woedde voort tot midden februari 1945 en eindigde met een geallieerde overwinning, zij het ten koste van zeer veel doden en gewonden aan beide kanten.

Op 27 januari 1945 verlieten de P-51 Mustangs van de 352 Fighter Group het vliegveld Y-29 Asch en werden ze op 8 februari 1945 vervangen door de 406 Fighter Group met P-47 Thunderbolts jachtvliegtuigen.

Vanaf Y-29 Asch werden de P-47 Thunderbolts ingezet voor luchtsteun tijdens de slag om de Rijn en de verdere opmars door Duitsland.

De afstand tussen Y-29 Asch en de vijandelijk doelen vergrootte met de opmars door Duitsland. Half april 1945 verhuisden hierdoor de 366 Fighter Group en de 406 Fighter Group naar het in Duitsland liggend Y-94 Handorf bij Münster.

Vanaf 16 april 1945 werd Y-29 Asch de thuisbasis van de 391 Bomber Group met A-26 Invader. Deze halfzware bommenwerpers voltooiden vanaf Y-29 Asch verschillende missies boven vijandelijk gebied zonder verliezen. De 391 Bomber Group vloog zijn laatste missie tijdens de Tweede Wereldoorlog vanaf Y-29 op 3 mei 1945.

Op 8 mei 1945 was de Tweede wereldoorlog in Europa voorbij en met de verhuizing op 27 mei 1945 van de 391 Bomber Group naar het vliegveld B-50 Vitry-en-Artois in Frankrijk betekende dit eveneens het einde van het Y-29 Asch.

Republic P-47D-22-RE Thunderbolt (42-26340) of the 391st Fighter Squadron (A8-F), 366th Fighter Group at Y-29 Asch. Nickname: "Fickle Flossy".

Photo: Heemkring Zutendaal

ALG Y-29 Asch, short history

Mid-September 1944 Zutendaal and environs were liberated by the Allies from four-year occupation by the Germans. But the war was not over yet. After the breakout from Normandy, the Allies advanced quickly but came to a halt at the German borders. It became very clear that the Germans would fiercely defend their country.

From 2nd to 21st October, 1944 there was the Battle of Aachen. During that time the Allies also wanted to invade the south east of Aachen, through the Hürtgenwald, further into Germany to capture the industrial area around the Ruhr River and then to reach the Rhine. In this area lay the Siegfried Line or Westwall.

The Ruhr River, flowing through the Hürtgenwald, was of great strategic importance to the Allies, particularly the dams in the river. The Germans were able to flood the Ruhr valley, sometimes up to 7.5 meters deep, so as to stop the Allied advance into Germany.

To get enough air support, it was decided on November 3rd, 1944 to build an airfield, Advanced Landing Ground, at Zutendaal. This would shorten the flight time from the airbase to the enemy target from one hour to fifteen minutes so that there was more time available over the enemy territory.

Two days later, on November 5th, 1944, the 852nd Engineer Aviation Battalion began the construction of the Advanced Landing Ground (ALG) Y-29. Located entirely within the territory of Wiemesmeer (township of Zutendaal), along the road from As to Bilzen, it got the name of the neighboring northern town Asch (now As).

In just three weeks the airfield was built, consisting of a single runway of 1500 meters which was built with PSP plates. These were steel plates, 3 meters long and 40 centimeters wide, provided with 3 rows of round holes so that the strength was preserved but still light enough to work with easily. Hooks and eyes were fitted on the sides so that each plate could be hooked together.

On 26th November 1944, the P-47 Thunderbolts fighters from the 366th Fighter Group landed at their new base. That same day the first missions from Y-29 Asch were flown towards the Hürtgenwald.

On December 16th, 1944, the Germans began the Battle of the Bulge. Thus, the fighting in the Hurtgenwald reduced temporarily. The missions from the Y-29 Asch then went direction the Ardennen. On December 23rd, 1994 the 352nd Fighter Group P-51 Mustang fighter planes were sent from Bodney (UK) to Y-29 Asch for reinforcement.

On January 1st, 1945 Y-29 Asch was attacked by dozens of German fighters during Operation Bodenplatte. This aerial combat will go down in history as "The Legend of Y-29", with a great success for the Allies.

After the failure of the Battle of the Bulge, the last great German offensive in the west, the Americans resumed the battle in Hürtgenwald on January 10th, 1945. This battle of the Hürtgenwald raged on until mid-February 1945 and ended with an Allied victory, albeit at the expense of a large number killed and injured from both sides.

On January 27th, 1945 the P-51 Mustangs of the 352nd Fighter Group left the Y-29 Asch and were replaced on February 8th, 1945 by the 406th Fighter Group P-47 Thunderbolts fighters.

From Y-29 Asch the P-47 Thunderbolts were used for air support during the Battle of the Rhine and the further advance through Germany.

The distance between Y-29 Asch and enemy targets increased with the advancement into Germany. Mid-April 1945 the 366th Fighter Group and the 406th Fighter Group moved to Y-94 in Münster near Handorf in Germany.

From April 16th, 1945 Y-29 Asch was the home for the 391st Bomber Group with the A-26 Invader. These light bombers completed from Y-29 Asch several missions over enemy territory without losses. On May 3rd, 1945 the 391st Bomber Group flew its last mission during World War II from Y-29.

On May 8th, 1945 the Second World War in Europe was over. The move on May 27th, 1945 of the 391 Bomber Group to B-50 Vitry-en-Artois in France marked the end of the Y-29 Asch.

Pilot Lt. Karl K. Dittmer in the North American P-51D-15-NA Mustang (44-14955) of the 487th Fighter Squadron (HO-I), 352nd Fighter Group at Y-29 Asch. Nickname: "Dopey Okie".

Photo: Heemkring Zutendaal

Y-29 Asch casualities by date

DATE	NAME	FIRST NAME	FIGHTER GROUP	SQUADRON	CEMETERY	PAGE
November 26, 1944	Cutshall	Edward	366	390	Tennessee, USA	10
November 26, 1944	Dunton	Wallace	366	390	California, USA	12
November 26, 1944	Wilson	Arthur	92 BG	327 BS	Margraten, NL	14
November 30, 1944	Aldrin	Roger	442TCG	305	Henri-Chapelle, B	16
November 30, 1944	Duffin	Bernard	442TCG	305	Henri-Chapelle, B	18
November 30, 1944	Leake	Farrer	442TCG	305	Henri-Chapelle, B	20
November 30, 1944	Simpson	George	442TCG	305	New Jersey, USA	22
November 30, 1944	Wright	Harold	442TCG	305	Henri-Chapelle, B	24
November 30, 1944	Smith	Philip	366	HQ	Pennsylvania, USA	26
December 1, 1944	Priddy	Henry	366	391	Margraten, NL	28
December 1, 1944	Stryker	Paul	366	391	Virginia, USA	30
December 16, 1944	Hall	Ivan	Roy. Can. Eng.	2Bat.B	Leopoldsburg, B	32
December 19, 1944	Colbroth	James	366	391	Henri-Chapelle, B	34
December 20, 1944	Boehm	Robert	366	389	North Dakota, USA	36
December 24, 1944	Jones	John	366	391	New Jersey, USA	38
December 24, 1944	McKinley	Albert	366	391	Massachusetts, USA	40
December 25, 1944	Johnson	Hilding	366	391	Neupré, B	42
December 25, 1944	Preddy	George	352	328	St Avold, F	44
December 26, 1944	Preece	Dennis	Royal Engineers		Leopoldsburg, B	46
December 26, 1944	Shorey	Frederick	Royal Engineers		Charleroi, B	48
December 26, 1944	Tafel	Carl	352	487	Kentucky, USA	50
December 27, 1944	Peterson	Elmer	366	389	California, USA	52
December 27, 1944	Steinfeld	Bernard	366	389	Luxembourg, L	54
December 31, 1944	Howard	Hugh	352	328	Kentucky, USA	56
January 1, 1945	Webber	Donald	183	RAF	Venray, NL	58
January 13, 1945	Earley	Joseph	366	389	Luxembourg, L	60
January 21, 1945	Aageberg	James	366	390	Henri-Chapelle, B	62
January 22, 1945	Hass	Floyd	366	391	Henri-Chapelle, B	64
January 24, 1945	Abbott	Earl	352	328	Cambridge, UK	66
February 13, 1945	Maloney	Keith	406	512	Neupré, B	68
February 20, 1945	Deja	Henry	406	512	Idaho, USA	70
February 20, 1945	Gildersleeve	John	406	514	Neupré, B	72
February 22, 1945	Ford	Alfred	406	512	Michigan, USA	74
February 22, 1945	Holland	George	406	514	Neupré, B	76
February 22, 1945	Spielman	Morgan	406	514	Indiana, USA	78
February 23, 1945	Graves	Richard	406	513	Neupré, B	80
February 23, 1945	Smart	Raymond	366	389	Margraten, NL	82
February 24, 1945	Marshall	William	69	RAF	Evere, B	84
February 24, 1945	Monaghan	James	69	RAF	Evere, B	86
February 24, 1945	Davies	William	69	RAF	Evere, B	88
February 25, 1945	Akin	John	406	512	Margraten, NL	90
February 28, 1945	Halterman	Claude	366	390	Margraten, NL	92
February 28, 1945	Kerlin	John	406	513	Pennsylvania, USA	94

DATE	NAME	FIRST NAME	FIGHTER GROUP	SQUADRON	CEMETERY	PAGE
March 1, 1945	Downs	Edward	366	389	Delaware, USA	96
March 1, 1945	McCauley	William	366	389	Alabama, USA	98
March 1, 1945	Pease	Stephen	366	389	Margraten, NL	100
March 1, 1945	Dean	Paul	784	Battery D	Tennessee, USA	102
March 9, 1945	Dufford	William	366	391	Arlington, USA	104
March 13, 1945	Beverly	Kenneth	366	391	Margraten, NL	106
March 14, 1945	Cobbe	Thomas	366	391	Margraten, NL	108
March 19, 1945	Mazal	Paul	406	513	Henri-Chapelle, B	110
March 21, 1945	McVay	James	406	514	Neupré, B	112
March 24, 1945	Fowler	Gordon	406	513	New Jersey, USA	114
March 25, 1945	Sweet	Bernard	406	514	Margraten, NL	116
March 26, 1945	Taylor	James	366	389	Margraten, NL	118
April 9, 1945	Stang	Alan	406	512	Illinois, USA	120
April 12, 1945	Bolle	John	406	513	St Avold, F	122

Republic P-47D Thunderbolts of the 366th Fighter Group at ALG Y-29 Asch.

Photo: Heemkring Zutendaal

IDENTIFICATION

Name: CUTSHALL
First name: EDWARD MATTHEWS
Born: June 2, 1923
Age: 21
Hometown: Limestone, Washington County, Tennessee, USA
Family: Bartley Chester Cutshall (father)
Lavada Shelton (mother)

Photo: find a grave

MILITARY SERVICE

Servicenumber: not available
Rank: 1st Lieutenant
Function: Pilot
Squadron: 390 Fighter Squadron
Group: 366 Fighter Group 9th Air Force

PLANE DATA

Serial number: 42-75436
Type: Republic P-47D-11-RE Thunderbolt

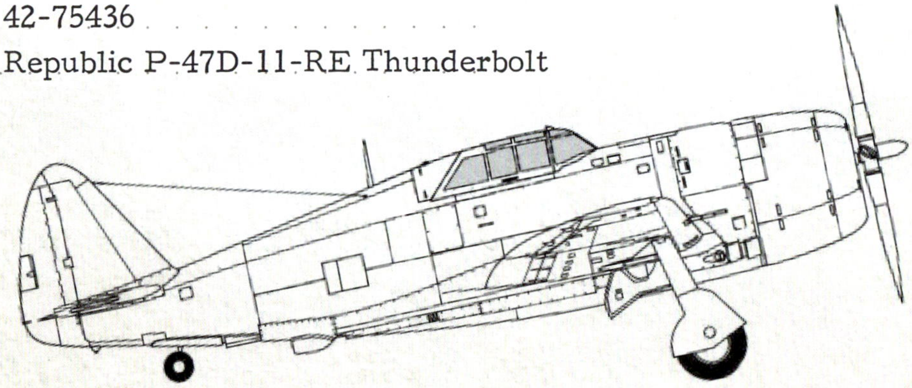

Registration: B2-
Nickname:
MACR: not available

CIRCUMSTANCE OF DECEASE

Date of death: November 26, 1944

Place of death: Birnbach, Germany

Cemetery: Happy Valley Memorial Park, Elizabethton, Carter County, Tennessee, USA

Gravenumber: Section: Crown, Plot 283, Grave 7

Headstone ABMC:

Other information: Approximately 100 German soldiers were seen dodging into the woods at Schleiden, Germany. Lt. Edward M Cutshall, on his first mission, was hit by 20 mm flak leaving the target; he tried to return to friendly territory before the engine quit. Apparently, he initially planned to stay with the plane and crash land it, but changed his mind as he got closer to the ground, at about 61 meters (200 feet) he attempted to bail out. The chute did not have time to open and he was killed. Plane reported found destroyed at Schmithof, Germany.

Memory Stone: EDWARD M. CUTSHALL
TENNESSEE
2 LIEUT. AIR CORPS
WORLD WAR II
JUNE 2 1923 - NOV 26 1944

Photo: find a grave

Photo: find a grave

IDENTIFICATION

Name: DUNTON
First name: WALLACE A. III
Born: May 16, 1924
Age: 20
Hometown: not available

Family: not available

MILITARY SERVICE

Servicenumber: not available
Rank: 1st Lieutenant
Function: Pilot
Squadron: 390 Fighter Squadron
Group: 366 Fighter Group 9th Air Force

PLANE DATA

Serial number: 42-75833
Type: Republic P-47D-11-RE Thunderbolt

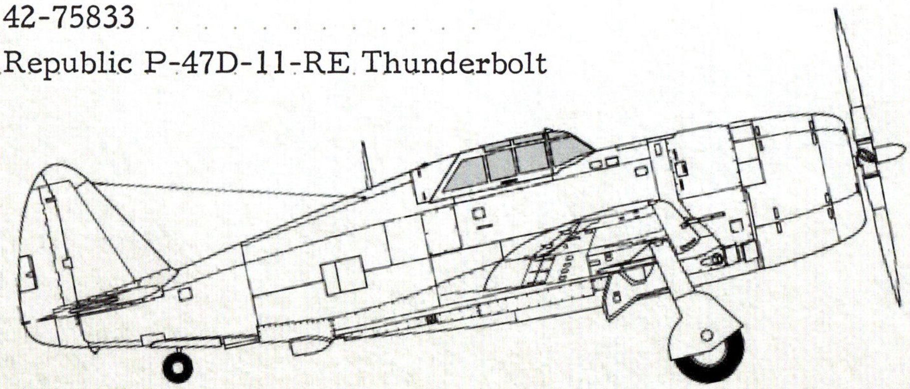

Registration: B2-
Nickname:
MACR: not available

CIRCUMSTANCE OF DECEASE

Date of death: November 26, 1944

Place of death: 3 miles south of Verviers, Belgium

Cemetery: Hollywood Forever Cemetery, Hollywood, Los Angeles County, California, USA

Gravenumber:

Headstone ABMC:

Other information: Eleven 390th T-Bolts were directed from Y-29 Asch to attack vehicles in Hassenfeld, Germany.
Lt. Wallace Dunton was hit by flak in the rear of the fuselage and caught fire. He and his wing man headed for friendly territory. By the time they crossed the front line, the intense flames had almost reached the radio compartment. Dunton, who was begged by his wing man to bail out, was last seen standing in the cockpit with flames closing in on him. He died in the crash 3 miles south of Verviers, Belgium.

Memory Stone: not available

Photos: find a grave

Photos: find a grave

IDENTIFICATION

Name:	WILSON
First name:	ARTHUR EVERETT
Born:	December 11, 1922
Age:	22
Hometown:	Westfield, Hampden County, Massachusetts, USA
Family:	Dennie G. Wilson (father)
	Ola M. (Hulbut) Wilson (mother)
	Charles D. Wilson (brother)
	Dorothy G. Wilson (sister)
	Kenneth A. Wilson (brother)
	Edward Wilson (brother)

MILITARY SERVICE

Servicenumber:	31284391		
Rank:	Staff Sergeant	Function:	Ball-turret gunner
Squadron:	327 Bomber Squadron	Group:	92 Bomber Group - 8th Air Force

PLANE DATA

Serial number:	42-31801
Type:	Boeing B-17G-30-BO Flying Fortress

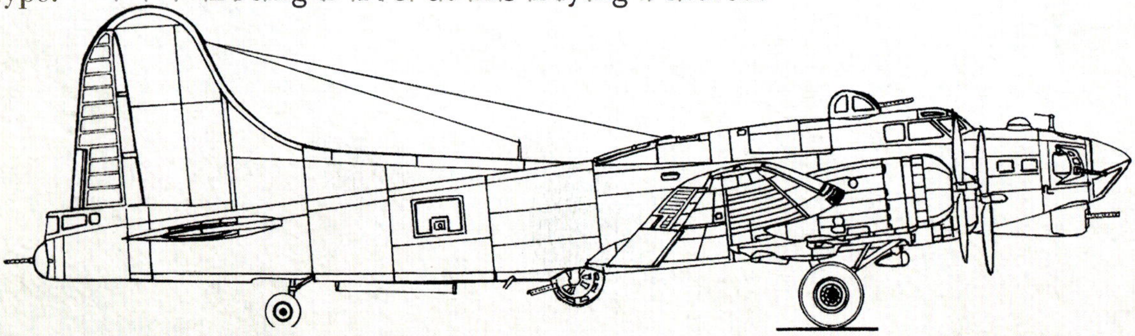

Registration:	UX-Q
Nickname:	
MACR:	not available

CIRCUMSTANCE OF DECEASE

Date of death: November 26, 1944

Place of death: Y-29 Asch, Belgium

Cemetery: Netherlands American Cemetery and Memorial, The Netherlands

Gravenumber: Plot N, Row 17, Grave 1

Headstone ABMC: ARTHUR E. WILSON
S. SGT 327 BOMB SQ 92 BOMB GP (H)
MASSACHUSETTS NOV 26 1944

Other information: The Boeing B-17G Flying Fortress 42-38101 was hit by flak above Germany. The plane made a emergency landing at Y-29 Asch with only one motor working. The ball-turret gunner Sgt. Arthur Wilson had been killed and several other crew members were wounded by German fire. The plane was left behind on the airfield.

Memory Stone: not available

Photo: Imperial War Museum

B-17 at ALG Y-29 Asch

Photo: find a grave

IDENTIFICATION

Name: ALDRIN
First name: ROGER LEON
Born: December 1, 1921
Age: 23
Hometown: Worcester County, Massachusetts, USA

Family: Elizabeth W.R. Aldrin (wife)
Gustav A. Aldrin (father)
Olga S. Aldrin (mother)

MILITARY SERVICE

Servicenumber: O-696531
Rank: 1st Lieutenant
Function: Pilot
Squadron: 305th Squadron
Group: 442nd Troop Carrier Group 9th AF

PLANE DATA

Serial number: 43-15131
Type: Douglas C-47A-80-DL Skytrain (DC-3)

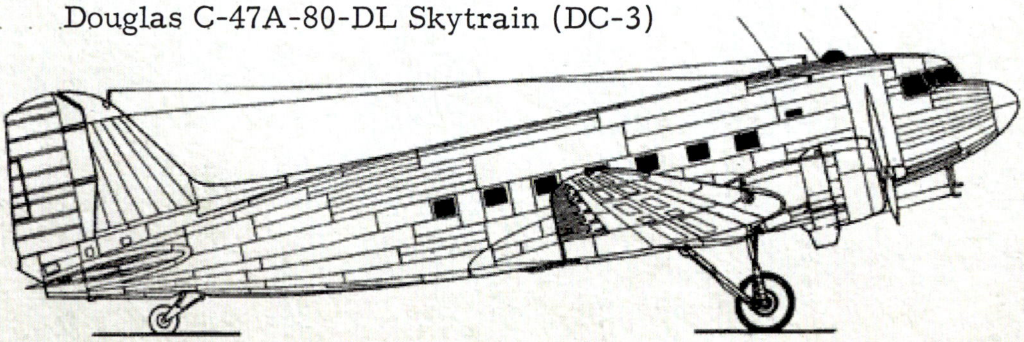

Registration: 4J
Nickname: Lady Eve
MACR: 10687

CIRCUMSTANCE OF DECEASE

Date of death: November 30, 1944

Place of death: Sivry-Rance, Belgium

Cemetery: Henri-Chapelle American Cemetery and Memorial, Belgium

Gravenumber: Plot G, Row 15, Grave 8

Headstone ABMC: ROGER L. ALDRIN
1 LT. 305 SQ 442 TRP CARR GR
MASSACHUSETTS NOV 30 1944

Other information: On course between Y-29 Asch and A-70 Laon/Couvron, France, the Douglas C-47 Skytrain aircraft, serial number 43-15131 piloted by First Lieutenant Roger L. Aldrin, had a mid air collision and crashed near Rance, Belgium. The other aircraft Douglas C-47 43-15122 landed safely.

Memory Stone:

IDENTIFICATION

Name: DUFFIN

First name: BERNARD PHILIP

Born: December 9, 1923

Age: 21

Hometown: San Antonio, Bexar County, Texas, USA

Family: Not available

Photo: find a grave

MILITARY SERVICE

Servicenumber: O-2062483

Rank: 2nd Lieutenant

Function: Copilot

Squadron: 305th Squadron

Group: 442nd Troop Carrier Group 9th AF

PLANE DATA

Serial number: 43-15131

Type: Douglas C-47A-80-DL Skytrain (DC-3)

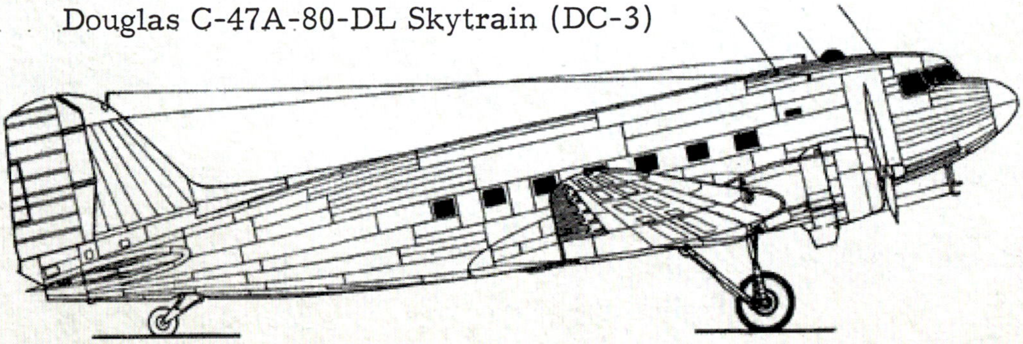

Registration: 4J

Nickname: Lady Eve

MACR: 10687

CIRCUMSTANCE OF DECEASE

Date of death: November 30, 1944

Place of death: Sivry-Rance, Belgium

Cemetery: Henri-Chapelle American Cemetery and Memorial, Belgium

Gravenumber: Plot B, Row 11, Grave 52

Headstone ABMC: BERNARD P. DUFFIN
2 LT 305 SQ 442 TRP CARR GP
TEXAS NOV 30 1944

Other information: On course between Y-29 Asch and A-70 Laon/Couvron, France, the Douglas C-47 Skytrain aircraft, serial number 43-15131 piloted by First Lieutenant Roger L. Aldrin, had a mid air collision and crashed near Rance, Belgium. The other aircraft Douglas C-47 43-15122 landed safely.

Memory Stone:

--- REGISTRATION FORM ---

IDENTIFICATION

Photo: find a grave

Name: SIMPSON
First name: GEORGE H.
Born: March 28, 1923
Age: 21
Hometown: Camden, New Jersey, USA

Family: George L Simpson (father)
Celia Simpson (mother)

MILITARY SERVICE

Servicenumber: 32755973
Rank: Sergeant **Function:** Crew Chief
Squadron: 305th Squadron **Group:** 442nd Troop Carrier Group 9th FA

PLANE DATA

Serial number: 43-15131
Type: Douglas C-47A-80-DL Skytrain (DC-3)

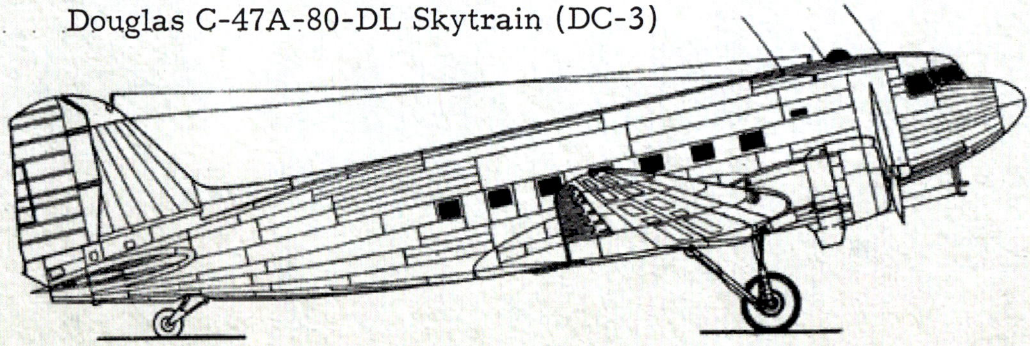

Registration: 4J
Nickname: Lady Eve
MACR: 10687

CIRCUMSTANCE OF DECEASE

Date of death: November 30, 1944
Place of death: Sivry-Rance, Belgium
Cemetery: Calvary Cemetery, Cherry Hill, Camden Country, New Jersey, USA
Gravenumber: ASN 32755973
Headstone ABMC:

Other information: On course between Y-29 Asch and A-70 Laon/Couvron, France, the Douglas C-47 Skytrain aircraft, serial number 43-15131 piloted by First Lieutenant Roger L. Aldrin, had a mid air collision and crashed near Rance, Belgium. The other aircraft Douglas C-47 43-15122 landed safely.

Memory Stone: GEORGE H SIMPSON
NEW JERSEY
SGT 442 AAF TRP CARRIER GP
WORLD WAR II
MARCH 28 1923 - NOV 30 1944

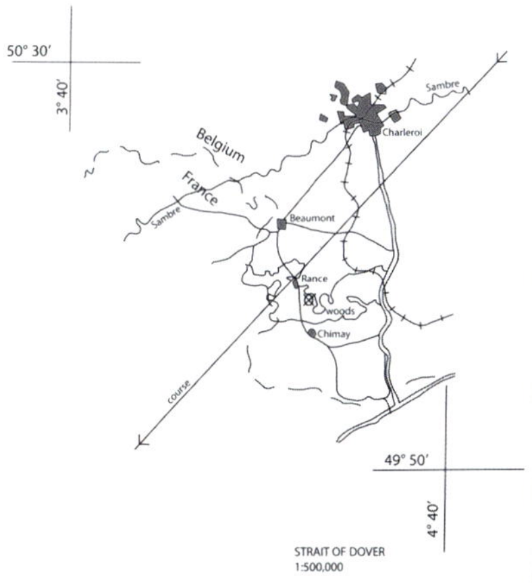

Photo: find a grave

IDENTIFICATION

Photo: find a grave

Name: WRIGHT
First name: HAROLD THOMAS
Born: September 28, 1920
Age: 24
Hometown: Los Angeles, California, USA

Family: Thomas S. Wright (father)
Ellen O. Wright (mother)
Lillian Wright (sister)
Samuel G. Wright (brother)
Robert Wright (brother)
Larry Wright (brother)
Madeline Wright (sister)
Ellen M. Wright (sister)

MILITARY SERVICE

Servicenumber: 39531873
Rank: Staff Sergeant
Function: Radio Operator
Squadron: 305th Squadron
Group: 442nd Troop Carrier Group 9th AF

PLANE DATA

Serial number: 43-15131
Type: Douglas C-47A-80-DL Skytrain (DC-3)

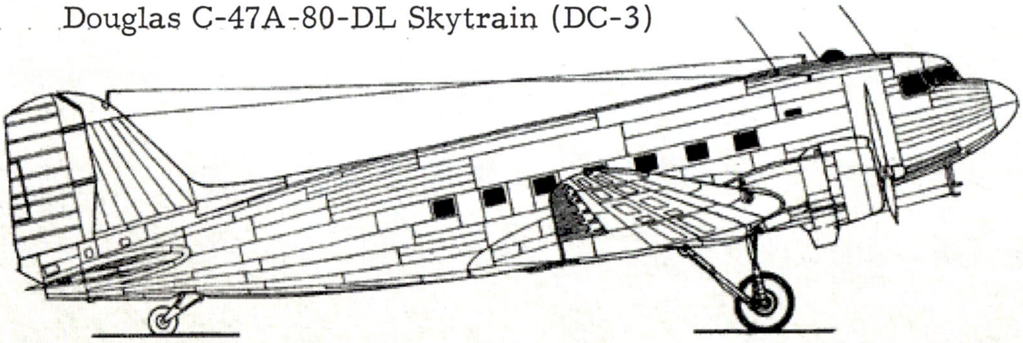

Registration: 4J
Nickname: Lady Eve
MACR: 10687

CIRCUMSTANCE OF DECEASE

Date of death:	November 30, 1944
Place of death:	Sivry-Rance, Belgium
Cemetery:	Henri-Chapelle American Cemetery and Memorial, Belgium
Gravenumber:	Plot H, Row 1, Grave 55
Headstone ABMC:	HAROLD T. WRIGHT S SGT 305 SQ 442 TRP CARR GP CALIFORNIA NOV 30 1944
Other information:	On course between Y-29 Asch and A-70 Laon/Couvron, France, the Douglas C-47 Skytrain aircraft, serial number 43-15131 piloted by First Lieutenant Roger L. Aldrin, had a mid-air collision and crashed near Rance, Belgium. The other aircraft Douglas C-47 43-15122 landed safely.

Memory Stone:

--- REGISTRATION FORM ---

IDENTIFICATION

Name: SMITH

First name: PHILIP MELVIN

Born: November 26, 1913

Age: 39

Hometown: Mount Lebanon, Allegheny County, Pennsylvania, USA

Family: Eleanor Pollit Smith (wife)
Ronaele Smith (daughter)
Philip S. Smith (father)
Mrs Philip S. Smith (mother)
Marshall L. Smith (brother)
Larry Wright (brother)
Madeline Wright (sister)
Ellen M. Wright (sister)

MILITARY SERVICE

Servicenumber: O-325527

Rank: Lieutenant Colonel

Function: Group Executive Officer

Squadron: Headquarters

Group: 366 Fighter Group - 9th Air Force

PLANE DATA

Serial number: 43-15131

Type: Douglas C-47A-80-DL Skytrain (DC-3)

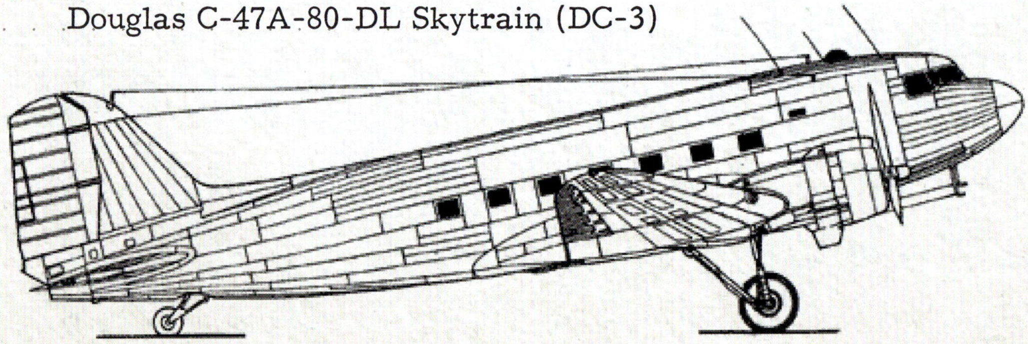

Registration: 4J

Nickname: Lady Eve

MACR: 10687

CIRCUMSTANCE OF DECEASE

Date of death:	November 30, 1944
Place of death:	Sivry-Rance, Belgium
Cemetery:	National Cemetery of the Alleghenies, Cecil, Washington County, Pennsylvania, USA
Gravenumber:	Section 7 site 1301
Headstone ABMC:	Temple of Love Mausoleum

Other information: Lieutenant Colonel Philip Smith was going back to the 366th's former base A-70 Laon/Couvron (France) for a final inspection of the facilities following the departure of the last of the Group's personnel and aircraft. He had a second important duty to perform on the trip. A secret "Pathfinder" bombsight had been left on the Y-29 by a B-17 bomber crew, which had made an emergency landing there. The plan was to deliver it directly to the proper 8th AAF authorities.
The Douglas C-47 Skytrain aircraft on course between Y-29 and A-70, piloted by 1st Lt. Roger Aldrin had a mid air collision near Rance, Belgium. Lieutenant Colonel Philip Smith was killed in the plane crash in which he was passenger.

Memory Stone:
PHILIP M SMITH
LT COL USAAF
WORLD WAR II
NOV 26 1913 NOV 30 1944
9TH AIR FORCE 366 FIGHTER GROUP

Photo: find a grave

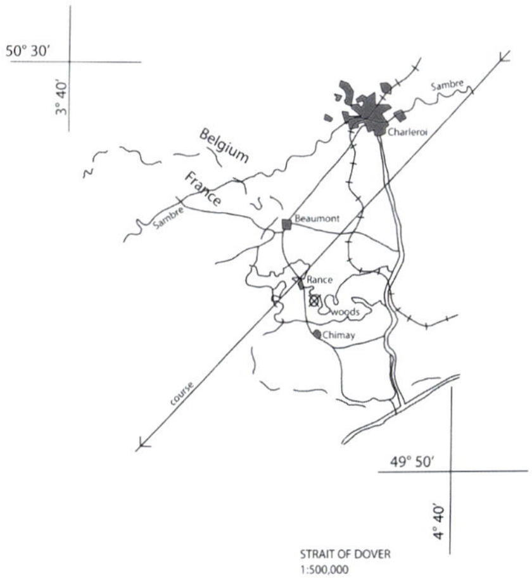

IDENTIFICATION

Photo: find a grave

Name: PRIDDY

First name: HENRY WASHINGTON

Born: April 12, 1907

Age: 37

Hometown: Charlotte County, Viginia, USA

Family: James Herbert Priddy (father)
Elizabeth L. (Lee) Priddy (mother)
Lovard L. (Crutchfield) Priddy (sister)
Oswald L. Priddy (brother)

MILITARY SERVICE

Servicenumber: 6796409

Rank: Private

Function: not available

Squadron: 391 Fighter Squadron

Group: 366 Fighter Group - 9th Air Force

~~PLANE DATA~~

Serial number: inapplicable

Type: inapplicable

Registration: inapplicable

Nickname: inapplicable

MACR: inapplicable

CIRCUMSTANCE OF DECEASE

Date of death: December 1, 1944
Place of death: not available
Cemetery: Netherlands American Cemetery and Memorial, The Netherlands.
Gravenumber: Plot O, Row 12, Grave 7
Headstone ABMC: HENRY W. PRIDDY
PVT 391 FTR SQ 366 FTR GP
VIRGINIA DEC 1 1944
Other information: Circumstances unknown.
He is also listed on the tombstone of his parents at the Merry Oaks Cemetery, Keysville, Charlotte County, Virginia, USA.

Memory Stone: PRIDDY
HENRY WASHINGTON
APR 12 1907 - DEC 19 1944
GAVE HIS LIFE FOR HIS COUNTRY
WORLD WAR II
BURIED IN U.S. CEMETERY
MARTRAGEN HOLLAND

Photo: find a grave

IDENTIFICATION

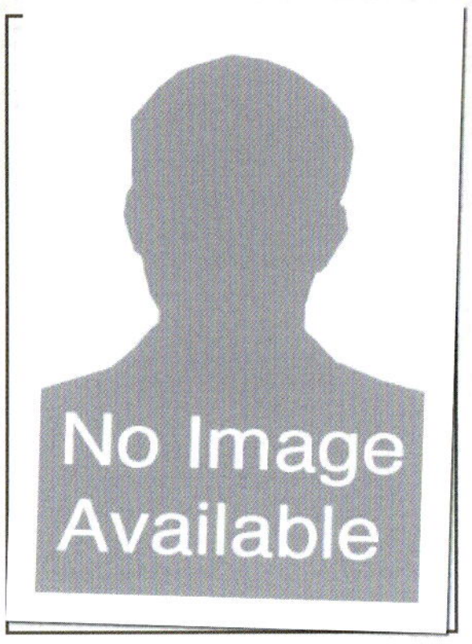

Name: STRYKER
First name: PAUL EDWARD JR
Born: March 24, 1924
Age: 20
Hometown: Henrico County, Virginia, USA

Family: Paul Edward Stryker (father)
Madeline (Costello) Stryker (mother)

MILITARY SERVICE

Servicenumber: not available
Rank: 1st Lieutenant
Function: Pilot
Squadron: 391 Fighter Squadron
Group: 366 Fighter Group - 9th Air Force

PLANE DATA

Serial number: 44-20416
Type: Republic P-47D-30-RE Thunderbolt

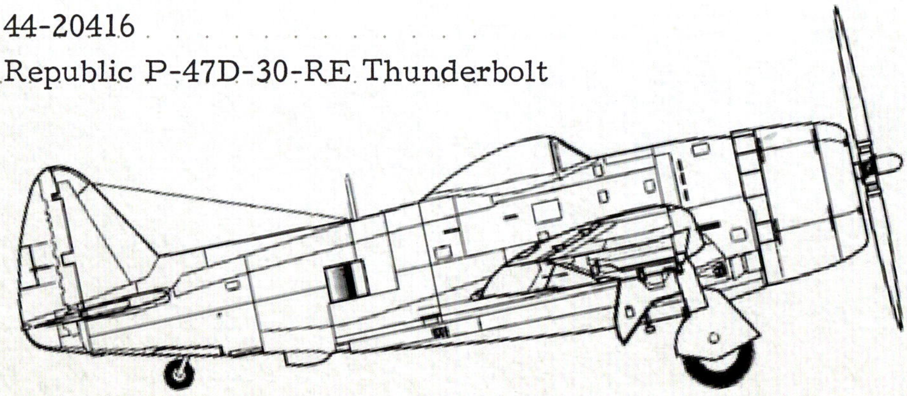

Registration: A8-
Nickname:
MACR: 10829

CIRCUMSTANCE OF DECEASE

Date of death: December 1, 1944

Place of death: Leversbach, Germany

Cemetery: Mount Calvary Cemetery, Richmond, Richmond City, Virginia, USA

Gravenumber: Section 5

Headstone ABMC:

Other information: Hit by flak while attacking enemy gun positions. Crashed and exploded at Leversbach, Germany.

Memory Stone: PAUL E. STRYKER JR
VIRGINIA
1 LIEUT AIR CORPS
WORLD WAR II
MARCH 24 1924 DEC 1 1944

Photo: find a grave

IDENTIFICATION

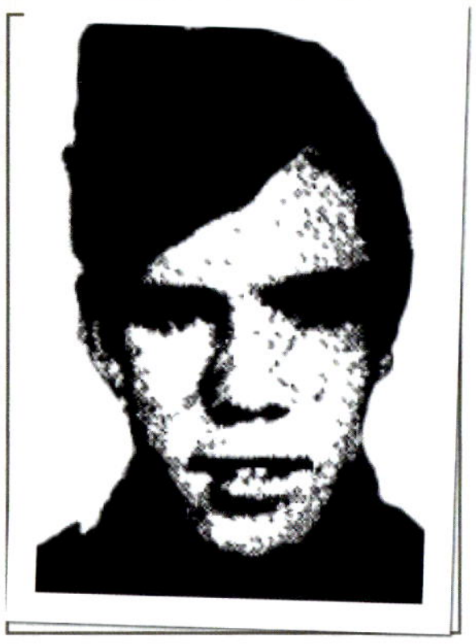

Photo: find a grave

Name: HALL
First name: IVAN
Born: July 23, 1923
Age: 21
Hometown: Toronto, Ontario, Canada

Family: Dorothy Rose Hall (Pascoe) (wife)
James Hall (father)
Agnes Hall (mother)
Donald Hall (brother)
Eileen Durante (Hall) (sister)

MILITARY SERVICE

Servicenumber: B.26958
Rank: Sapper **Function:**
Squadron: Royal Canadian Engineers **Group:** 2 Battalion, B Company

---

~~PLANE DATA~~

Serial number: inapplicable
Type: BSA M20 motorcycle

Registration: inapplicable
Nickname:
MACR: inapplicable

CIRCUMSTANCE OF DECEASE

Date of death: December 16, 1944

Place of death: Lanklaar (Dilsen-Stokkem), Belgium

Cemetery: Leopoldsburg War Cemetery, Belgium

Gravenumber: VI. A. 4

Headstone ABMC: B.26958
I. HALL
CORPS OF
ROYAL CANADIAN ENGINEERS
16TH DECEMBER 1944 AGE 22
TILL MEMORY FADES
AND LIFE DEPARTS
YOU WILL LIVE
FOREVER IN OUR HEARTS

Other information: On December 16, 1944, sapper Ivan Hall was dispatched to go from Paal (Beringen, Belgium) to Papenhoven (Grevenbicht, The Netherlands) riding a motor-cycle for the purpose of picking up mail and canteen supplies. On his way back he was accidentally killed in a collision with a US Army truck.
The truck, a Diamond "T" 4 ton 6x6 dump truck of the 852nd Engineer Aviation Battalion, was on his way to a gravel pit between As and Lanklaar (Belgium) to pick up gravel for Y-29 Asch. Sapper Ivan Hall first was buried in a temporary cemetery located at a point 1 ½ miles North West of Eisden (Maasmechelen), Belgium. Reburied in October 1946 at the Leopoldsburg War Cemetery, Belgium.

Memory Stone:

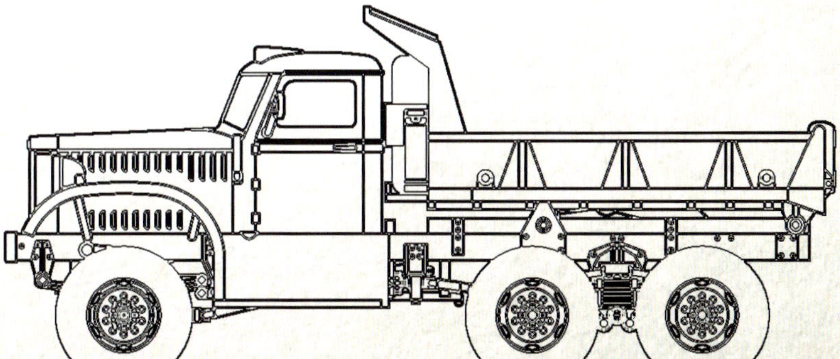

Diamond "T" 4 ton 6x6

- - - REGISTRATION FORM - - -

IDENTIFICATION

Name: COLBROTH
First name: JAMES MERVYN
Born: June 14, 1922
Age: 22
Hometown: Sonoma County, California, USA

Family: Harry W. Colbroth (father)
Mary B. (Hornbuckle) Colbroth (mother)
Mervyn F. Colbroth (adopted brother)
Virginia Lee (fiancee)

MILITARY SERVICE

Servicenumber: O-763497
Rank: 1st Lieutenant Function: Pilot
Squadron: 391 Fighter Squadron Group: 366 Fighter Group - 9th Air Force

PLANE DATA

Serial number: 44-20251
Type: Republic P-47D-28-RE Thunderbolt

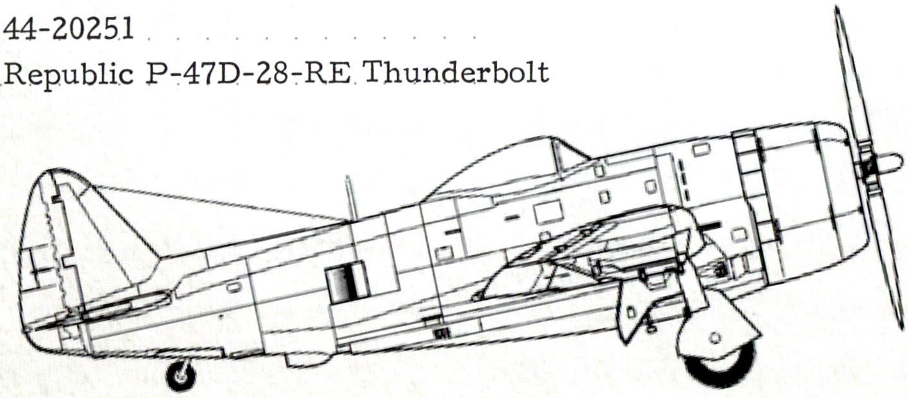

Registration: A8-H
Nickname:
MACR: 11019

CIRCUMSTANCE OF DECEASE

Date of death: December 19, 1944

Place of death: Ferschweiler, Germany

Cemetery: Henri-Chapelle American Cemetery and Memorial, Belgium

Gravenumber: Plot E, Row 16, Grave 38

Headstone ABMC: JAMES M. COLBROTH
1 LT 391 FTR SQ 366 FTR GP
CALIFORNIA DEC 19 1944

Other information: Lt James Colbroth with his aircraft A8-H was last seen while bombing a target. Hit by flak at Ferschweiler, Germany. Black smoke was seen rising from the hill in front of the target.

Memory Stone:

IDENTIFICATION

Name: BOEHM
First name: ROBERT FREDERICK "JERRY" JR
Born: December 4, 1924
Age: 20
Hometown: Turtle Lake, McLean County, North Dakota, USA
Family: Robert Frederick Boehn (father)
Mary Eliza (Perrine) Boehn (mother)
Willa Brink Boehm (sister)

Photo: find a grave

MILITARY SERVICE

Servicenumber: O-774000
Rank: 2nd Lieutenant
Function: Pilot
Squadron: 389 Fighter Squadron
Group: 366 Fighter Group - 9th Air Force

PLANE DATA

Serial number: 44-20294
Type: Republic P-47D-28-RE Thunderbolt

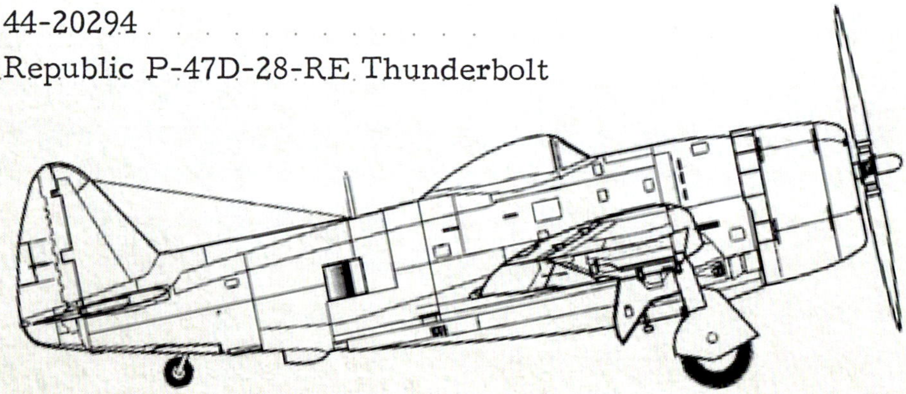

Registration: A6-
Nickname:
MACR: not available

CIRCUMSTANCE OF DECEASE

Date of death: December 20, 1944

Place of death: A-89 Le Culot, Belgium

Cemetery: Highland Home Cemetery, Jamestown, Stutsman County, North Dakota, USA

Gravenumber: Div A, Sec Q, Block 18, Grave 7

Headstone ABMC:

Other information: Alert Flight on December 19, 1944. They were vectored to the Duren, Germany, area to intercept reported enemy fighters. No enemy aircraft were encountered. Three ships returned to Y-29 and found the runway practically invisible. With the assistance of the Control Tower unit, two were "talked down" safely. Lt Angove, the third 389th pilot, nosed aver at the end of the runway. His T-Bolt was written off inventory as not repairable (Category E). The other eight P-47 landed at site A-89 Le Culot. Two 389th pilots collided on the runway at A-89 as they were making their roll-out: Lt Elmer Peterson (P-47 42-27230) escaped without injuries, but Lt. Robert Boehm (P-47 44-20294) was seriously injured and died in the hospital the next day (December 20, 1944).

Memory Stone: "JERRY"
LT.ROBERT F.BOEHM,JR.
DEC. 4, 1924
DEC. 20, 1944

Photo: find a grave

IDENTIFICATION

Name: JONES
First name: JOHN KESSLER
Born: October 29, 1924
Age: 20
Hometown: Nebraska, USA

Family: not availble

Photo: find a grave

MILITARY SERVICE

Servicenumber: O-830232
Rank: 2nd Lieutenant
Function: Pilot
Squadron: 391 Fighter Squadron
Group: 366 Fighter Group - 9th Air Force

PLANE DATA

Serial number: 42-26278
Type: Republic P-47D-22-RE Thunderbolt

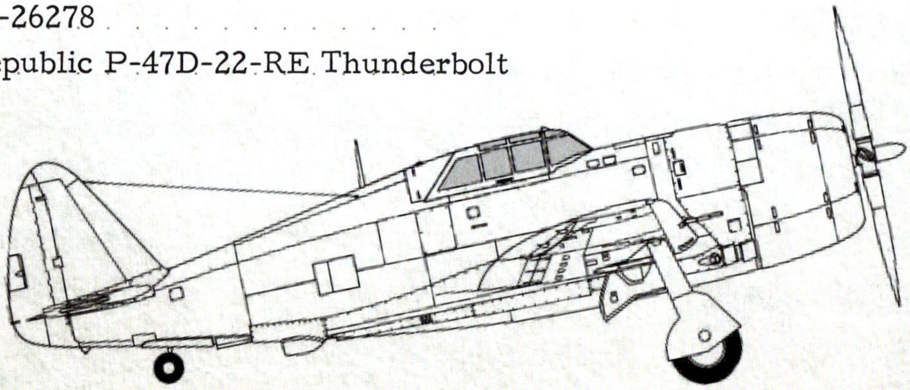

Registration: A8-Y
Nickname: Lil Herbie
MACR: 11412

CIRCUMSTANCE OF DECEASE

Date of death: December 24, 1944

Place of death: Ahrweiler, Germany

Cemetery: Fairview Cemetery, Westfield, Union County, New Jersey, USA

Gravenumber: Div A, Sec Q, Block 18, Grave 7

Headstone ABMC:

Other information: The Alert Flight took off in response to a warning from the controller: a formation of Luftwaffe fighters was heading west from their bases east of the Rhine River. The 366th pilots' flight path intersected with that of the seventy-five Messerschmitt Me109s and Focke-Wulf FW190s flying at 9144 meters (30.000 feet) over Duren, Germany. 2nd Lieutenant John Jones was shot down near Ahrweiler, Germany by a Messerschmitt Me109.

Memory Stone: not availble

Photo: find a grave

- - - REGISTRATION FORM - - -

IDENTIFICATION

Name: PREECE
First name: DENNIS GEORGE
Born: not available
Age: 20
Hometown: United Kingdom

Family: not available

MILITARY SERVICE

Servicenumber: 14363442
Rank: Sapper
Function:
Squadron: 249 Airborne Field Company
Group: Royal Engineers UK

~~PLANE DATA~~

Serial number: inapplicable
Type: inapplicable

Registration: inapplicable
Nickname:
MACR: inapplicable

CIRCUMSTANCE OF DECEASE

Date of death: December 26, 1944

Place of death: Wiemesmeer (Zutendaal), Belgium

Cemetery: Leopoldsburg War Cemetery, Belgium

Gravenumber: VIII. B. 13

Headstone ABMC: 14363442 SAPPER
D.G. PREECE
ROYAL ENGINEERS
AIRBORNE
26TH DECEMBER 1944 AGE 20

Other information: On December 26, 1944, the Germans subjected the Y-29 airfield to a serious night-bombing and -strafing attack. During the night they made four separate attacks with antipersonnel bombs and cannon-fire strafing, the first at 19:18 and the last at 23:30. At the airfield Y-29 they caused minor damage and wounded several personnel, only one seriously, but they killed two British soldiers in Wiemesmeer (Zutendaal) that bore the brunt of one bombing.

Memory Stone:

- - - REGISTRATION FORM - - -

Photo: paradata.org.uk

IDENTIFICATION

Name: SHOREY

First name: FREDERICK GEORGE

Born: not available

Age: 22

Hometown: North Shields, Northumberland, UK

Family: John Shorey (father)
Dorothy Shorey (mother)

MILITARY SERVICE

Servicenumber: 2156029

Rank: Sapper

Function:

Squadron: 249 Airborne Field Company

Group: Royal Engineers UK

~~PLANE DATA~~

Serial number: inapplicable

Type: inapplicable

Registration: inapplicable

Nickname:

MACR: inapplicable

CIRCUMSTANCE OF DECEASE

Date of death: December 26, 1944

Place of death: Wiemesmeer (Zutendaal), Belgium

Cemetery: Charleroi Communal Cemetery, Charleroi, Belgium

Gravenumber: 22 Row V. Grave 27

Headstone ABMC: 2156029 SAPPER
F.G. SHOREY
ROYAL ENGINEERS
AIRBORNE
26TH DECEMBER 1944 AGE 22
IN GODS GARDEN NOW AT REST
PEACEFULLY SLEEPING
LIES ONE OF THE BEST

Other information: On December 26, 1944, the Germans subjected the Y-29 airfield to a serious night-bombing and -strafing attack. During the night they made four separate attacks with antipersonnel bombs and cannon-fire strafing, the first at 19:18 and the last at 23:30. At the airfield Y-29 they caused minor damage and wounded several personnel, only one seriously, but they killed two British soldiers in Wiemesmeer (Zutendaal) that bore the brunt of one bombing.

Memory Stone:

Photo: find a grave

Photo: find a grave

--- REGISTRATION FORM ---

Photo: find a grave

IDENTIFICATION

Name: TAFEL
First name: CARL GEORGE JR
Born: March 25, 1920
Age: 24
Hometown: Louisville, USA

Family: Carl George Tafel (father)
Edna Sargent Tafel (mother)

MILITARY SERVICE

Servicenumber: O-706469
Rank: 1st Lieutenant
Function: Pilot
Squadron: 487 Fighter Squadron
Group: 352 Fighter Group - 8th Air Force

PLANE DATA

Serial number: 44-13953
Type: North American P-51D-5-NA Mustang

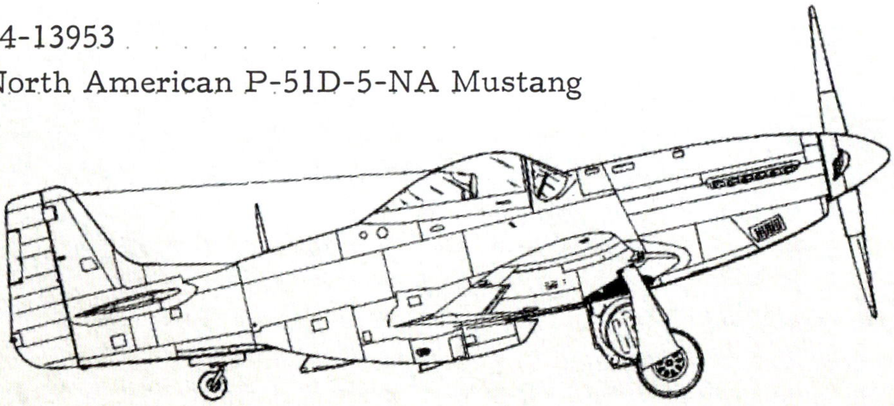

Registration: HO-
Nickname:
MACR: 11086

CIRCUMSTANCE OF DECEASE

Date of death:	December 26, 1944
Place of death:	Liers (Hönningen), Germany
Cemetery:	Cave Hill Cemetery, Louisville, Jefferson County, Kentucky, USA
Gravenumber:	
Headstone ABMC:	

Other information: On December 26, 1944, the 487th dove to assist a formation of P-47s being attacked by Me-109s west of Bonn. The group's intelligence section filed a report the following day: "Lt Tafel, flying with Capt. Hamilton, with squadron engaged ten-plus Me-109s. His plane was seen to get hit and catch on fire." Tafel was shot down and killed. His aircraft crashed near Liers, Germany, and the Germans buried his body in the cold ground next to the wreckage.

Memory Stone:
CARL GEORGE TAFEL JR.
SON OF CARL GEORGE AND EDNA SARGENT TAFEL
BORN MAR. 25, 1920
LIEUTENANT U.S. ARMY AIR FORCE
PILOT - 487TH FIGHTER SQUADRON
KILLED IN ACTION - LIERS, GERMANY DEC. 26, 1944

Photo: find a grave

Photo: find a grave

IDENTIFICATION

Photo: find a grave

Name: PETERSON
First name: ELMER R.
Born: May 4, 1924
Age: 20
Hometown: Colfax, USA

Family: Jarl R. Peterson (father)
Susie C. Peterson (mother)

MILITARY SERVICE

Servicenumber: O-767355
Rank: 2nd Lieutenant
Function: Pilot
Squadron: 389 Fighter Squadron
Group: 366 Fighter Group - 9th Air Force

PLANE DATA

Serial number: 44-20093
Type: Republic P-47D-28-RE Thunderbolt

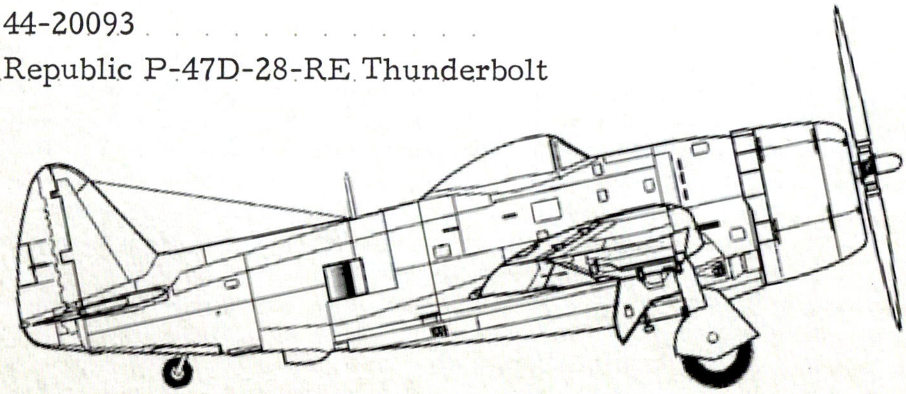

Registration: A6-
Nickname:
MACR: 11472

CIRCUMSTANCE OF DECEASE

Date of death: December 27, 1944

Place of death: Habscheid, Germany

Cemetery: Colfax Cemetery, Colfax, Placer County, California, USA

Gravenumber:

Headstone ABMC:

Other information: A dogfight in the vicinity of Habscheid, Germany, was taking place at all levels over a wide area when the 389th squadron entered the battle at the 8000 foot level. Lt Elmer R. Peterson was last been seen in the vicinity of Robertville, Belgium, attacking the enemy.
He was originially buried in a US Military cemetery in southeastern Belgium before being brought home and buried in the Colfax Cemetery.

Memory Stone: ELMER R PETERSON
WASHINGTON
2D LIEUT 366 AAF FIGHTER SQ
WORLD WAR II
MAY 4 1924 DEC 27 1944

Photo: find a grave

IDENTIFICATION

Name: STEINFELD
First name: BERNARD J.
Born: March 28, 1924
Age: 20
Hometown: Pennsylvania, USA

Family: not available

MILITARY SERVICE
Servicenumber: O-830572
Rank: 2nd Lieutenant
Function: Pilot
Squadron: 389 Fighter Squadron
Group: 366 Fighter Group - 9th Air Force

PLANE DATA
Serial number: 44-28517
Type: Republic P-47D-28-RA Thunderbolt

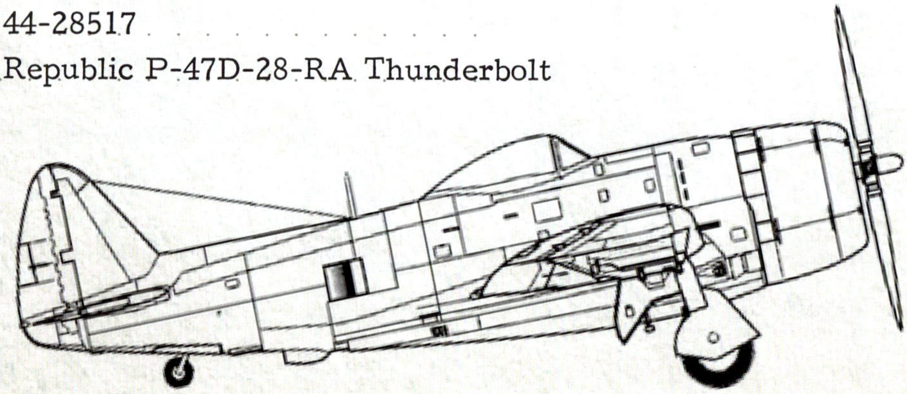

Registration: A6-
Nickname:
MACR: 11473

CIRCUMSTANCE OF DECEASE

Date of death:	December 27, 1944
Place of death:	Habscheid, Germany
Cemetery:	Luxembourg American Cemetery and Memorial, Luxembourg
Gravenumber:	Plot C, Row 6, Grave 25
Headstone ABMC:	BERNARD J. STEINFELD 2 LT 389 FTR SQ 366 FTR GP PENNSYLVANIA DEC 27 1944
Other information:	A dogfight in the vicinity of Habscheid, Germany, was taking place at all levels over a wide area when the 389th squadron entered the battle at the 8000 foot level. Lt Bernard J. Steinfeld was last been seen in the vicinity of Robertville, Belgium, attacking the enemy.

Memory Stone:

IDENTIFICATION

Name:	HOWARD
First name:	HUGH ASHER JR
Born:	July 10, 1924
Age:	20
Hometown:	Knox County, Kentucky, USA
Family:	Bonnie Jean Martin (wife)
	Hugh Howard (father)
	Chelsea (Marsee) Howard (mother)
	James Howard (brother)

MILITARY SERVICE

Servicenumber:	not available		
Rank:	flight officer	Function:	Pilot
Squadron:	328 Fighter Squadron	Group:	352 Fighter Group - 8th Air Force

PLANE DATA

Serial number:	44-13759
Type:	North American P-51D-5-NA Mustang

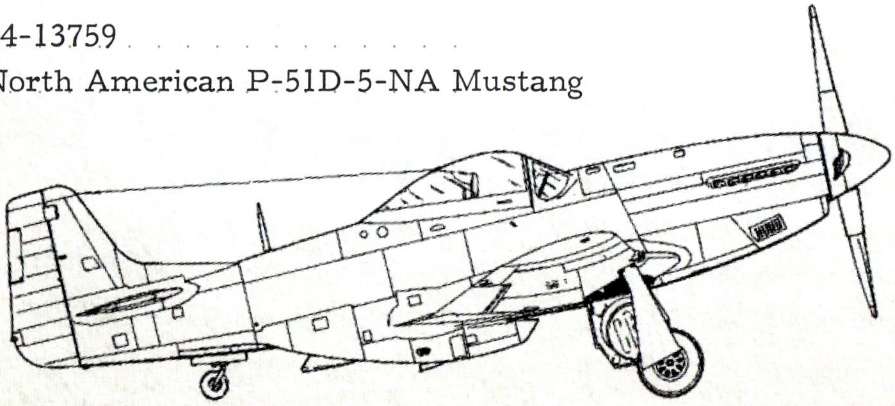

Registration:	PE-K
Nickname:	Lonesome Polecat
MACR:	11456

CIRCUMSTANCE OF DECEASE

Date of death: December 31, 1944

Place of death: 4 miles South of Ostend, Belgium

Cemetery: Barbourville Cemetery, Barbourville, Knox County, Kentucky, USA

Gravenumber:

Headstone ABMC:

Other information: Crashed 4 miles South of Ostend, Belgium, due to bad weather conditions during a transfer flight from Bodney, United Kingdom, to Y-29 Asch, Belgium.

Memory Stone: HUGH ASHER HOWARD JR
KENTUCKY
FLT O 352 AAF FIGHTER GP
WORL WAR II
JULY 10 1924 DEC 31 1944

Photo: find a grave

IDENTIFICATION

Name: WEBBER
First name: DONALD D.
Born: 1913
Age: 31
Hometown: Bowden, Cheshire, UK

Family: Winifred Margaret Webber (wife)
William John Webber (father)
Maria Elizabeth Webber (mother)

MILITARY SERVICE

Servicenumber: 138091
Rank: Flight Lieutenant
Function: Pilot
Squadron: 183 Squadron
Group: Royal Air Force Volunteer Reserve

PLANE DATA

Serial number: EK497
Type: Hawker Typhoon 1b

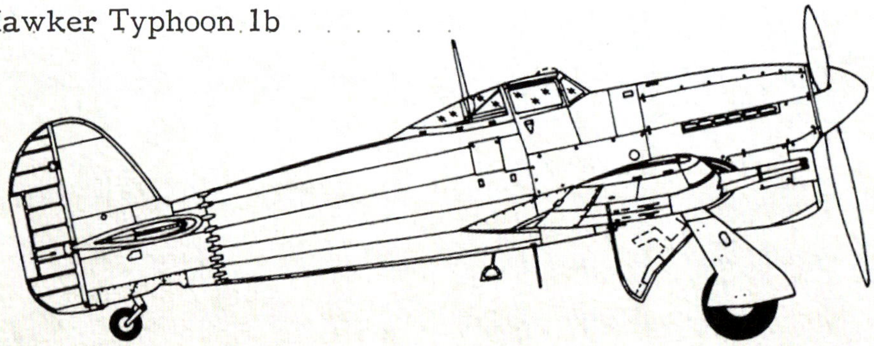

Registration: HF-E
Nickname:
MACR: inapplicable

CIRCUMSTANCE OF DECEASE

Date of death: January 1, 1945

Place of death: Y-29 Asch

Cemetery: Venray War Cemetery, The Netherlands

Gravenumber: VIII. F. 3.

Headstone ABMC: FLIGHT LIEUTENANT
D. WEBBER
PILOT
ROYAL AIR FORCE
1ST JANUARY 1945 AGE 31
"... DEATH HAS MADE
HIS DARKNESS BEAUTIFUL
WITH THEE"

Other information: The flying control reported German fighters at the base area of Y-29 and the 328th squadron (352 Fighter Group) returned to base in search of bandits. Lt Hill shot down a Hawker Typhoon which was identified, in the confusion, as a Focke-Wulf FW-190. Lt Hill said everybody was talking on the radio and hollering "bandits". He lined up on this one and gave a short burst. Immediately he sadly knew what he had done.

Memory Stone:

Photo: aircrewremembered.com

IDENTIFICATION

Photo: fields of honor

Name: EARLEY
First name: JOE C.
Born: May 29, 1920
Age: 24
Hometown: Fairfield, Iowa, USA

Family: Dorothy Clair Walton (wife)
Nancy Earley (daughter)
John William Earley (father)
Minnie B. Campbell Earley (mother)
Nancy Joan Earley (sister)

MILITARY SERVICE

Servicenumber: O-429505
Rank: Major
Function: Pilot
Squadron: 389 Fighter Squadron
Group: 366 Fighter Group - 9th Air Force

PLANE DATA

Serial number: 42-27230
Type: Republic P-47D-27-RE Thunderbolt

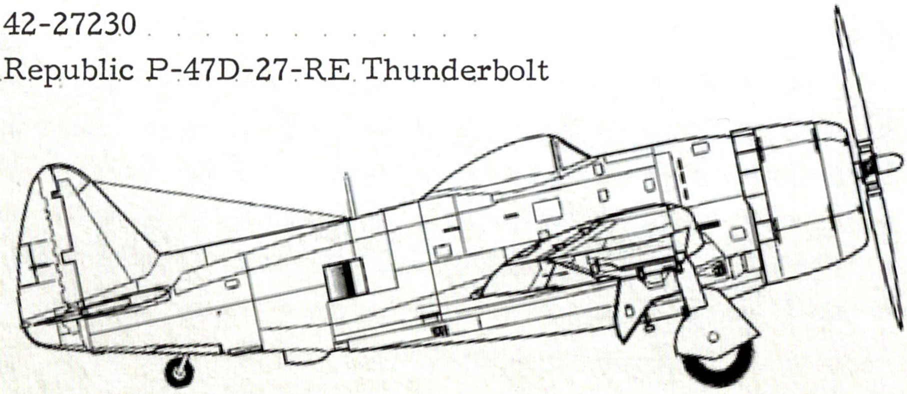

Registration: A6-
Nickname:
MACR: 11929

CIRCUMSTANCE OF DECEASE

Date of death:	January 13, 1945
Place of death:	Gouvy, Belgium
Cemetery:	Luxembourg American Cemetery and Memorial, Luxembourg
Gravenumber:	Plot E, Row 4, Grave 28
Headstone ABMC:	JOE C. EARLEY MAJ 389 FTR SQ 366 FTR GP IOWA JAN 13 1945
Other information:	Fighter Pilot, Major Joe C. Earley crashed January 13 1945 at 12.40 hours, 2 miles west of Gouvy, Belgium. Major Earley was #3 in a four ship flight of P-47D Thunderbolt. He was shot down by flak as he dove to low altitude to identify suspected enemy vehicles on road near Gouvy. A memorial to Major Joe Earley was erected at Gouvy, Belgium, near the spot he crashed.
Memory Stone:	WE REMEMBER MAJOR JOE C. EARLEY IOWA

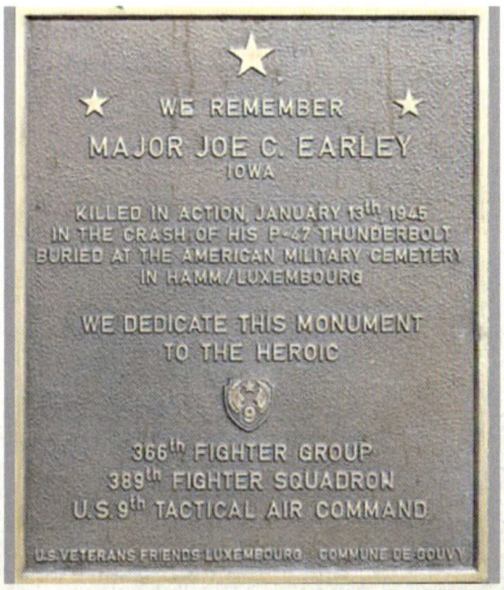

Photo: find a grave

- - - REGISTRATION FORM - - -

IDENTIFICATION

Name: AAGEBERG
First name: JAMES BLAINE
Born: July 10, 1924
Age: 20
Hometown: Hammond, Lake County, Indiana, USA

Photo: find a grave

Family:
Mabel I. (Robbins) Aageberg (wife)
Adler C. Aageberg (father)
Alice (Sexton) Aageberg (mother)
Richard Aageberg (brother)
Ruth P. Aageberg (sister)
Russell E. Aageberg (brother)
Arthur Aageberg (brother)

MILITARY SERVICE

Servicenumber: O-813104
Rank: Captain
Function: Pilot
Squadron: 390 Fighter Squadron
Group: 366 Fighter Group - 9th Air Force

PLANE DATA

Serial number: 44-20424
Type: Republic P-47D-30-RE Thunderbolt

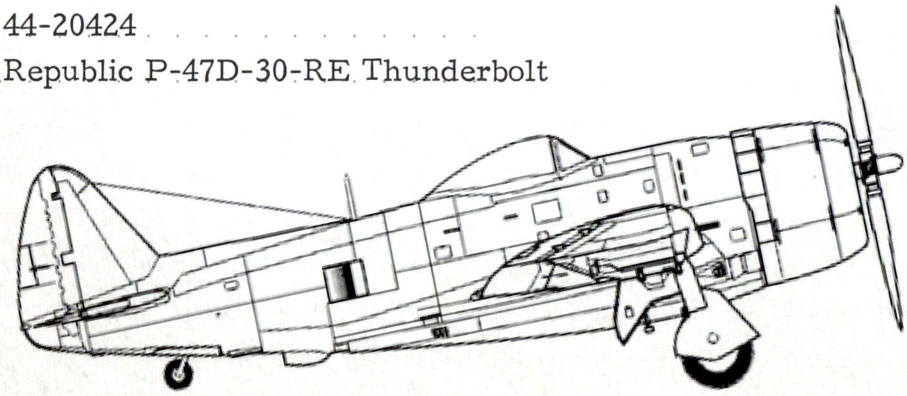

Registration: B2-
Nickname:
MACR: 11783

CIRCUMSTANCE OF DECEASE

Date of death: January 21, 1945

Place of death: Burtonville, Belgium

Cemetery: Henri-Chapelle American Cemetery and Memorial, Belgium

Gravenumber: Plot C Row 1 Grave 39

Headstone ABMC: JAMES B. AAGEBERG
CAPT 390 FTR GP 366 FTR GP
INDIANA JAN 21 1945

Other information: While leading a strafing run, Lt. James Aageberg's engine was hit by accurate intense light flak. While it was still running, he and his wing man headed west for the American lines west of Vielsalm, Belgium. As he was fighting to gain altitude it lost power, and although he was still over enemy occupied soil, he elected to bail out. The wing man started to follow him down as he left the plummeting plane but when the parachute deployed and it didn't blossom, he pulled out of his downward spiral and watched in horror as Lt Aageberg hit in a patch of woods at Burtonville, two miles east of Vielsalm, Belgium.

Memory Stone:

Photo: Photo: fields of honor

IDENTIFICATION

Photo: find a grave

Name: HASS
First name: FLOYD NATHANIEL
Born: September 27, 1921
Age: 20
Hometown: Chadron, Nebraska, USA

Family: Alice “Peggy” (Adams) Hass (wife)
Nathaniel Hass (father)
Clara A. (Weiland) Hass (mother)
Miriam A. Hass (sister)
Walter C. Hass (brother)
Alvin W. Hass (brother)
Francis Hass (brother)
Gordon Hass (brother)
Edith M. Hass (sister)

MILITARY SERVICE

Servicenumber: O-770264
Rank: 1st Lieutenant
Function: Pilot
Squadron: 391 Fighter Squadron
Group: 366 Fighter Group - 9th Air Force

PLANE DATA

Serial number: 42-76464
Type: Republic P-47D-20-RE Thunderbolt

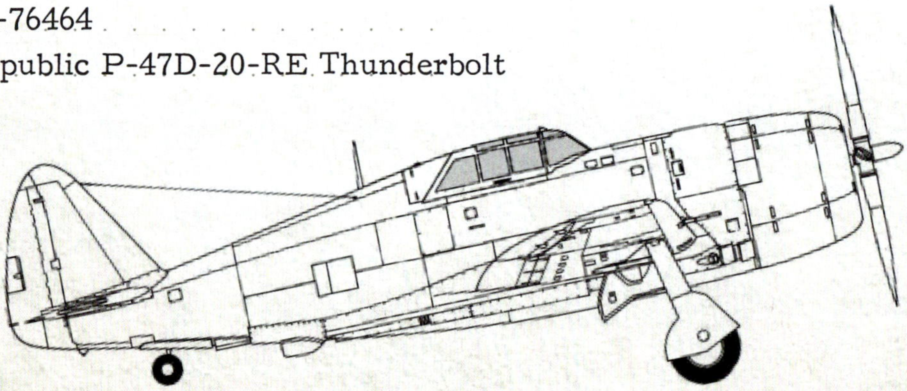

Registration: A8-O
Nickname: Peg O'My Heart
MACR: not available

CIRCUMSTANCE OF DECEASE

Date of death:	January 22, 1945
Place of death:	Malmedy, Belgium
Cemetery:	Henri-Chapelle American Cemetery and Memorial, Belgium
Gravenumber:	Plot F, Row 4, Grave 3
Headstone ABMC:	FLOYD N. HASS 1 LT 391 FTR GP 366 FTR GP NEBRASKA JAN 22 1945
Other information:	Lts. F. Hass and R.D. Hunt were to ascertain the cloud cover conditions over the fluid front. Northeast of Malmedy, Belgium, Lt. Hass reduced his altitude to check the actual ceiling versus those reported. He crashed with his P-47D-30 Thunderbolt into the hillside near the front lines. The name Peg O'My Heart was written on the nose of the plane. It was based on the name of the pilot's young bride, Peggy, and a popular Irish song.

Memory Stone:

Photo: find a grave

- - - REGISTRATION FORM - - -

IDENTIFICATION

Photo: fields of honor

Name:	GILDERSLEEVE
First name:	JOHN ROBINSON JR
Born:	April 2, 1916
Age:	28
Hometown:	McDowell County, West Virginia, USA
Family:	John R. Gildersleeve (father) Laura (Beavers) Gildersleeve (mother)

MILITARY SERVICE

Servicenumber: O-353421

Rank: Captain — Function: Pilot

Squadron: 514 Fighter Squadron — Group: 406 Fighter Group - 9th Air Force

PLANE DATA

Serial number: not available

Type: Republic P-47D Thunderbolt

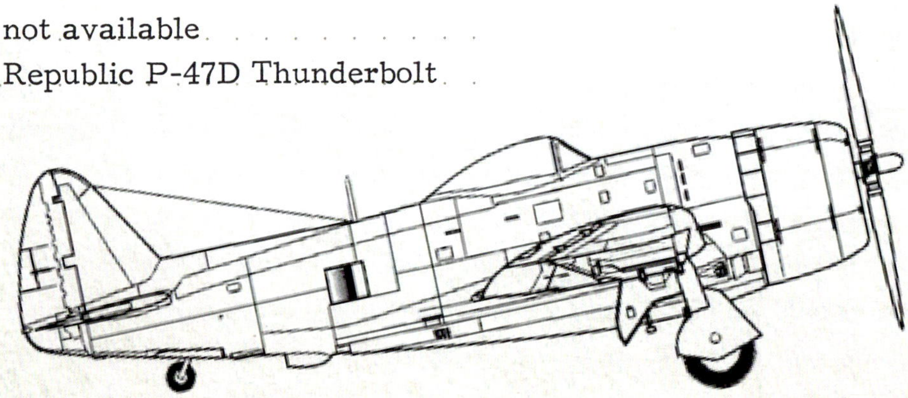

Registration: O7-

Nickname:

MACR: 12553

CIRCUMSTANCE OF DECEASE

Date of death: February 20, 1945

Place of death: not available

Cemetery: Ardennes American Cemetery and Memorial, Belgium

Gravenumber: Plot C, Row 16, Grave 12

Headstone ABMC: JOHN R. GILDERSLEEVE JR
CAPT 514 FTR SQ 406 FTR GP
WEST VIRGINIA FEB 20 1945

Other information: His plane was lost on the way from Burtonwood (England) to Y-29. Lt Porter, Capt. Gildersleeve and Lt Henry M. Deja started out from Burtonwood England, to ferry planes to Y-29. The weather was very bad and Lt Porter became separated from Capt. Gildersleeve and Lt Deja. That was the last Lt Porter saw of the other two officers.
There is a memory stone at the Maplewood Cemetery, Tazewell, Tazewell County, Virginia, USA.

Memory Stone: CAPT J.R. GILDERSLEEVE JR
BORN APRIL 2, 1916
DIED IN ACTION E.T.O.
FEB. 20, 1945

Photo: find a grave

--- REGISTRATION FORM ---

Photo: find a grave

IDENTIFICATION

Name: FORD

First name: ALFRED BRUSH

Born: November 27, 1921

Age: 23

Hometown: Grosse Pointe, Wayne County, Michigan, USA

Family: Frederick Clifford Ford (father)
Virginia Brush Ford (mother)

MILITARY SERVICE

Servicenumber: O-707677

Rank: 1st Lieutenant — Function: Pilot

Squadron: 512 Fighter Squadron — Group: 406 Fighter Group - 9th Air Force

PLANE DATA

Serial number: 44-33048

Type: Republic P-47D-30-AR Thunderbolt

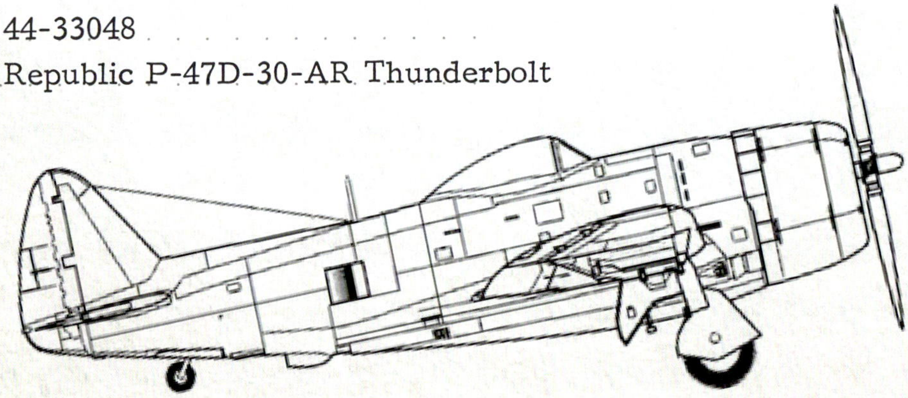

Registration: L3-

Nickname:

MACR: 12696

CIRCUMSTANCE OF DECEASE

Date of death: February 22, 1945

Place of death: Ascheberg, Germany

Cemetery: Elmwood Cemetery, Detroit, Wayne County, Michigan, USA

Gravenumber:

Headstone ABMC:

Other information: Shot down during an air battle by Messerschmitt Bf 109K-4 flown by Fw. Gunther Tschertner of JG 27/13 at Ascheberg, Southwest of Münster, Germany

Memory Stone:
ALFRED BRUSH FORD
SON OF
FREDERICK CLIFFORD AND VIRGINIA BRUSH FORD
1ST. LIEUT. U.S. AIR FORCE - FIGHTER PILOT
BORN AT GROSSE POINTE, MICH., NOV.27, 1921
KILLED IN COMBAT
OVER ASCHEBERG, GERMANY FEB. 22, 1945
WORLD WAR II

Photo: find a grave

Photo: find a grave

- - - REGISTRATION FORM - - -

IDENTIFICATION

Name: HOLLAND
First name: GEORGE HERMAN
Born: March 4, 1921
Age: 24
Hometown: Cochise County, Arizona, USA

Family: John W. Holland Sr. (father)
Frances P. (Brill) Holland (mother)
John W. Holland (brother)
Edward J. Holland (brother)
Frank D. Holland (brother)
Anna M. Holland (sister)
Estell M. Holland (sister)
Joseph H. Holland (brother)

MILITARY SERVICE

Servicenumber: O-762509
Rank: 1st Lieutenant   Function: Pilot
Squadron: 514 Fighter Squadron   Group: 406 Fighter Group - 9th Air Force

PLANE DATA

Serial number: 44-20583
Type: Republic P-47D-30-RE Thunderbolt

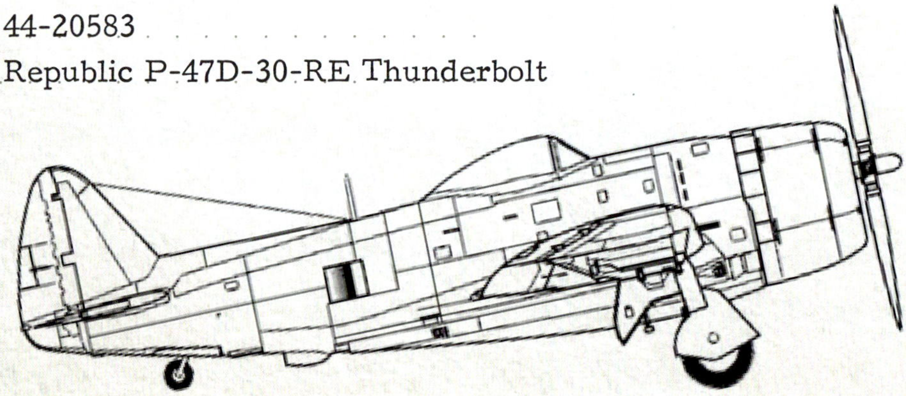

Registration: O7-
Nickname:
MACR: 12694

CIRCUMSTANCE OF DECEASE

Date of death: February 22, 1945

Place of death: Rheda, Germany

Cemetery: Ardennes American Cemetery and Memorial, Belgium

Gravenumber: Plot B, Row 42, Grave 22

Headstone ABMC: GEORGE H. HOLLAND
1 LT 514 FTR SQ 406 FTR GP
ARIZONA FEB 22 1945

Other information: Shot down during an air battle by Messerschmitt Bf 109K-4 believed flown by Ofw. Heinz Polak (his 6th victory) of JG 53/11 northeast of Rheda, Germany.

Memory Stone:

IDENTIFICATION

Name: SPIELMAN
First name: MORGAN JR
Born: December 2, 1922
Age: 22
Hometown: not available

Family: not available

MILITARY SERVICE

Servicenumber: O-826793
Rank: 1st Lieutenant
Function: Pilot
Squadron: 514 Fighter Squadron
Group: 406 Fighter Group - 9th Air Force

PLANE DATA

Serial number: 44-20252
Type: Republic P-47D-28-RE Thunderbolt

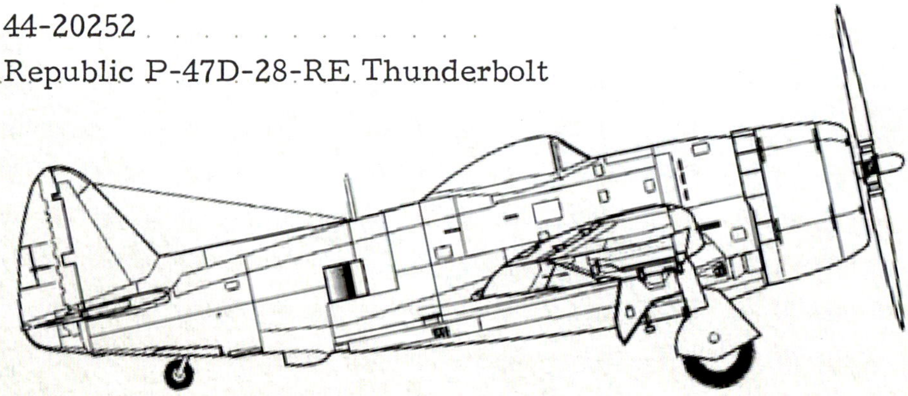

Registration: O7-
Nickname: “VD”
MACR: 12693

CIRCUMSTANCE OF DECEASE

Date of death: February 22, 1945

Place of death: Rheda, Germany

Cemetery: Greenlawn Memorial Park, Fort Wayne, Allen County, Indiana, USA.

Gravenumber:

Headstone ABMC:

Other information: Shot down during an air battle by Messerschmitt Bf 109K-4 believed flown by Ofw. Heinz Polak (his 7th victory) of JG 53/11 northeast of Rheda, Germany.

Memory Stone: LIEUTENANT
MORGAN SPIELMAN, JR
DEC.2, 1922 FEB. 2, 1945
514TH. FIGHTER SQUADRON, 406TH. GROUP
9TH. AIR FORCE
DIED IN GERMANY

Photo: find a grave

IDENTIFICATION

Photo: fields of honor

Name: GRAVES
First name: RICHARD DORSEY
Born: October 13, 1916
Age: 28
Hometown: Pierce County, Washington, USA

Family: Mary Virginia (Kalleberger) Graves (wife)
Harry T. Graves (father)
Frances O. (Dorsey) Graves (mother)
Frank T. Graves (brother)

MILITARY SERVICE

Servicenumber: O-427497
Rank: Major **Function:** Pilot
Squadron: 513 Fighter Squadron **Group:** 406 Fighter Group - 9th Air Force

PLANE DATA

Serial number: 44-20398
Type: Republic P-47D-30-RE Thunderbolt

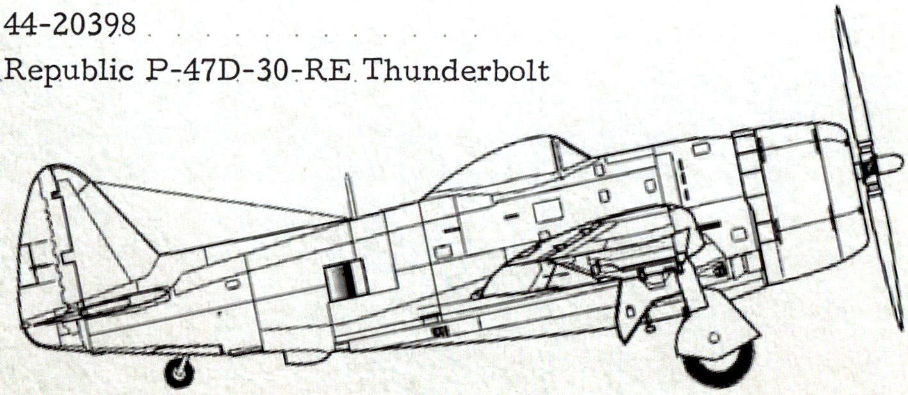

Registration: 4P-
Nickname:
MACR: 12640

CIRCUMSTANCE OF DECEASE

Date of death:	February 23, 1945
Place of death:	Between Ratingen and Hessel, Germany
Cemetery:	Ardennes American Cemetery and Memorial, Belgium
Gravenumber:	Plot B, Row 34, Grave 47
Headstone ABMC:	RICHARD D. GRAVES MAJ 513 FTR SQ 406 FTR GP WASHINGTON FEB 23 1945
Other information:	Shot down by flak while strafing vehicles on an autobahn between Ratingen and Hessel, Germany.

Memory Stone:

Photo: find a grave

IDENTIFICATION

Photo: find a grave

Name: SMART
First name: RAYMOND ELMER JR
Born: June 4, 1918
Age: 26
Hometown: Longmeadow, Hampden County, Massachusetts, USA
Family:
Betty J. (Houck) Smart (wife)
Raymond E. Smart (father)
Christine (Bolter) Smart (mother)
Elwin R. Smart (brother)
Ralph P. Smart (brother)
Harold E. Smart (brother)

MILITARY SERVICE

Servicenumber: O-024419
Rank: Major
Function: Pilot
Squadron: 389 Fighter Squadron
Group: 366 Fighter Group - 9th Air Force

PLANE DATA

Serial number: 44-20540
Type: Republic P-47D-30-RE Thunderbolt

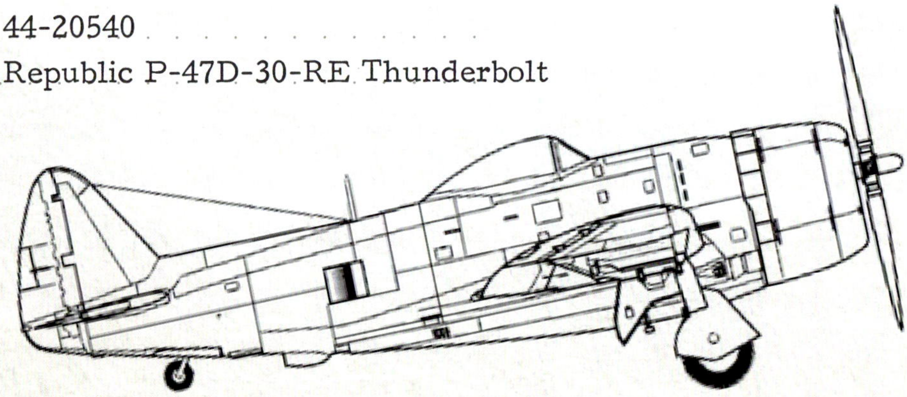

Registration: A6-
Nickname:
MACR: 12641

CIRCUMSTANCE OF DECEASE

Date of death: February 23, 1945

Place of death: Grevenbroich, Germany

Cemetery: Netherlands American Cemetery and Memorial, The Netherlands

Gravenumber:

Headstone ABMC: Plot N, Row 21, Grave 13
RAYMOND E. SMART JR
MAJ 389 FTR SQ 366 FTR GP
MASSACHUSETTS FEB 23 1945

Other information: He was hit by flak and crashed while the flight was circling over a rail target about three miles southeast of Grevenbroich, northwest of Cologne, Germany. He was first reported missing in action 23 February 1945.

Memory Stone:

- - - REGISTRATION FORM - - -

IDENTIFICATION

Photo: Christopher Marshall

Name: MARSHALL
First name: WILLIAM HAROLD
Born: December 8, 1921
Age: 23
Hometown: Ashton, Makerfield, Lancashire, UK

Family: Gwendoly Joan Marshall (wife)
Christopher Marshall (son)
William Marshall (father)
Clara Hill (mother)

MILITARY SERVICE

Servicenumber: 1684879
Rank: Sergeant
Function: Pilot
Squadron: 69 Squadron
Group: 34 Wing - Royal Air Force

PLANE DATA

Serial number: not available
Type: Vickers Wellington XIII

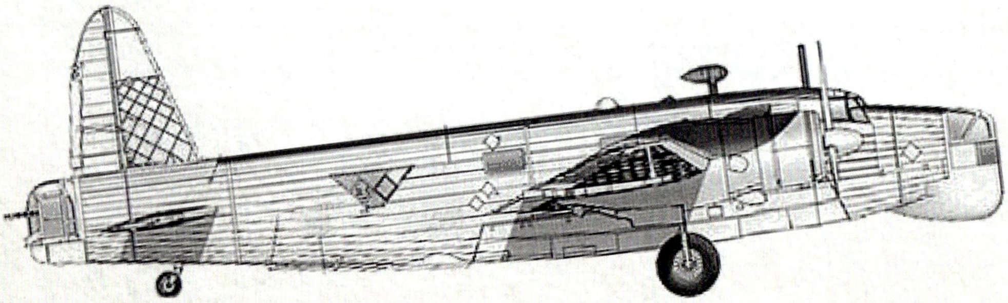

Registration: NC604
Nickname:
MACR: inapplicable

CIRCUMSTANCE OF DECEASE

Date of death: February 24, 1945

Place of death: Waterschei, Genk, Belgium

Cemetery: Brussels Town Cemetery, Belgium

Gravenumber: X.27.58

Headstone ABMC: 1684879 SERGEANT
W.H. MARSHALL
PILOT
ROYAL AIR FORCE
24TH FEBRUARY 1945 AGE 24
HIS SMILES, HIS COURAGE,
HIS BOUNTEOUS LOVE
WERE WORTHIER
OF A PLACE ABOVE

Other information: The Vickers Wellington XIII NC604 night reconnaissance, was hit by a German night fighter above Wassenberg, Germany. The pilot managed to fly the crippled airplane back to friendly territory, but was hit by the anti-aircraft defences of the Y-29. Two crew members jumped out the plane and came down with their parachute. The plane, with the other three crew members in it, went down and crashed at Waterschei (Genk), Belgium.

Memory Stone:

Photo: Christopher Marshall

Photo: Luc Meyvis

Photo: Christopher Marshall

IDENTIFICATION

Name: MONOGHAN
First name: JAMES CARSON
Born: not available
Age: 21
Hometown: Dalbeattie, Kirkcudbrightshire, UK

Family: James Scott Monaghan (father)
Margaret Carson Monaghan (mother)

MILITARY SERVICE

Servicenumber: 1568242
Rank: Sergeant
Function: Navigator
Squadron: 69 Squadron
Group: 34 Wing - Royal Air Force

PLANE DATA

Serial number: not available
Type: Vickers Wellington XIII

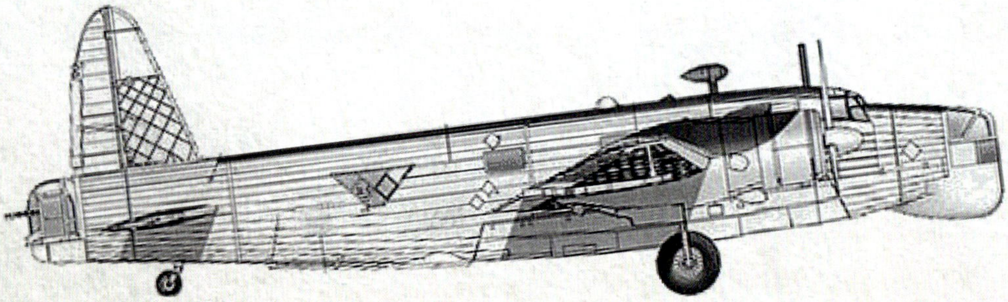

Registration: NC604
Nickname:
MACR: inapplicable

CIRCUMSTANCE OF DECEASE

Date of death: February 24, 1945

Place of death: Waterschei, Genk, Belgium

Cemetery: Brussels Town Cemetery, Belgium

Gravenumber: X.27.57

Headstone ABMC: 1568242 SERGEANT
J.C. MONAGHAN
NAVIGATOR
ROYAL AIR FORCE
24TH FEBRUARY 1945 AGE 21
ALWAYS IN OUR THOUGHTS
HE DIED THAT WE MIGHT LIVE

Other information: The Vickers Wellington XIII NC604 night reconnaissance, was hit by a German night fighter above Wassenberg, Germany. The pilot managed to fly the crippled airplane back to friendly territory, but was hit by the anti-aircraft defences of the Y-29. Two crew members jumped out the plane and came down with their parachute. The plane, with the other three crew members in it, went down and crashed at Waterschei (Genk), Belgium.

Memory Stone:

Photo's: Luc Meyvis

The three crewmembers of the Wellington NC604 side by side at the Brussels Town Cemetery

IDENTIFICATION

Name: DAVIES

First name: WILLIAM ERIC

Born: not available

Age: not available

Hometown: not available

Family: not available

MILITARY SERVICE

Servicenumber: 1675418

Rank: Sergeant

Function: Air Gunner

Squadron: 69 Squadron

Group: 34 Wing - Royal Air Force

PLANE DATA

Serial number: not available

Type: Vickers Wellington XIII

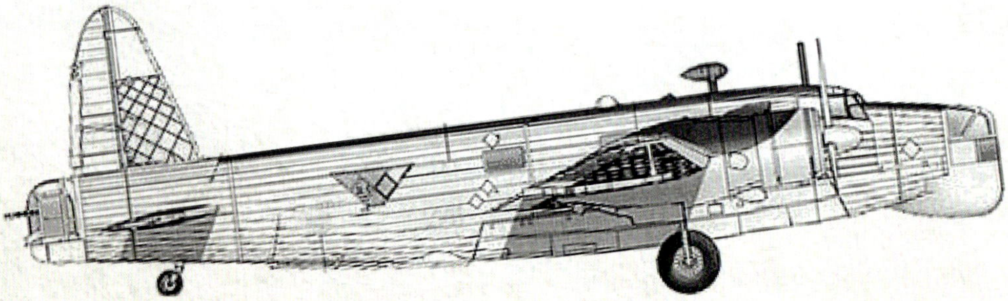

Registration: NC604

Nickname:

MACR: inapplicable

CIRCUMSTANCE OF DECEASE

Date of death: February 24, 1945

Place of death: Waterschei, Genk, Belgium

Cemetery: Brussels Town Cemetery, Belgium

Gravenumber: X.27.56

Headstone ABMC: 1675418 SERGEANT
W.E. DAVIES
AIR GUNNER
ROYAL AIR FORCE
24TH FEBRUARY 1945

Other information: The Vickers Wellington XIII NC604 night reconnaissance, was hit by a German night fighter above Wassenberg, Germany. The pilot managed to fly the crippled airplane back to friendly territory, but was hit by the anti-aircraft defences of the Y-29. Two crew members jumped out the plane and came down with their parachute. The plane, with the other three crew members in it, went down and crashed at Waterschei (Genk), Belgium.

Memory Stone:

Photo: Luc Meyvis

The three crewmembers of the Wellington NC604 side by side at the Brussels Town Cemetery
Photo: Christopher Marshall

IDENTIFICATION

Photo: find a grave

Name: HALTERMAN
First name: CLAUDE ALLEN JR
Born: May 14, 1922
Age: 22
Hometown: Satacoy, Ventura County, California, USA

Family: Claude A. Halterman (father)
Bertha M. (Berry) Halterman (mother)
Floyd L. Halterman (brother)
Lula M. Halterman (sister)
Kenneth G. Halterman (brother)
Betty L. Halterman (sister)

MILITARY SERVICE

Servicenumber: O-767204
Rank: 1st Lieutenant   Function: Pilot
Squadron: 390 Fighter Squadron   Group: 366 Fighter Group - 9th Air Force

PLANE DATA

Serial number: 42-29148
Type: Republic P-47D-28-RA Thunderbolt

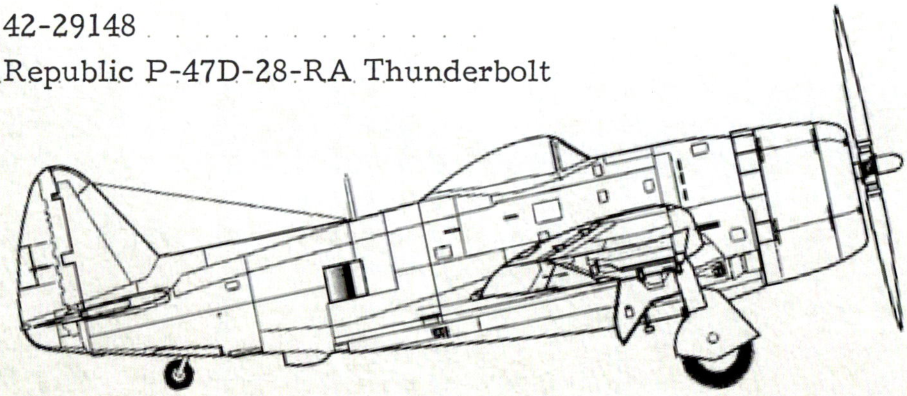

Registration: B2-A
Nickname:
MACR: 12798

CIRCUMSTANCE OF DECEASE

Date of death:	February 28, 1945
Place of death:	Morgensternsheide, Germany
Cemetery:	Netherlands American Cemetery and Memorial, The Netherlands
Gravenumber:	Tablets of the Missing
Headstone ABMC:	HALTERMAN CLAUDE A JR 1LT 390 FTR SQ 366 FTR GP CALIFORNIA

Other information: The plane of 1st Lieutenant Claude Halterman was hit by flak near Grevenbroich. He tried to bail out but could not make it. The plane augered in Morgensternsheide, about 2½ miles north of Grevenbroich. His body was never recovered.

Memory Stone:

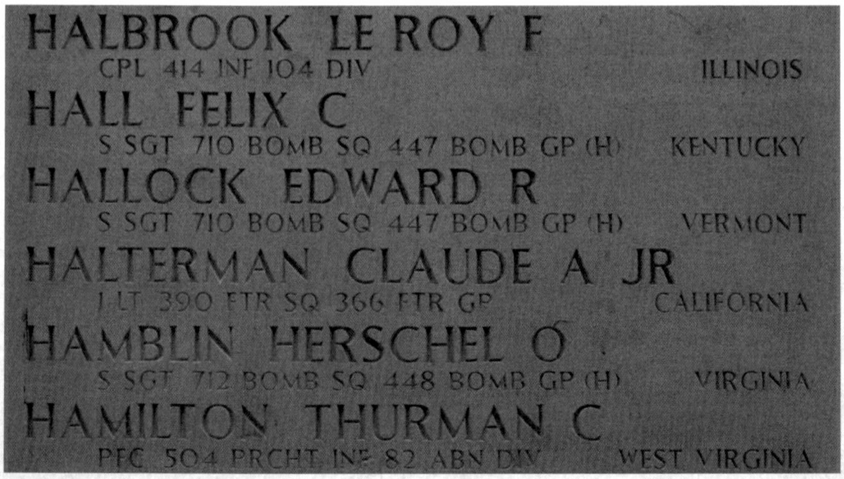

Photo: find a grave

- - - REGISTRATION FORM - - -

IDENTIFICATION

Name: KERLIN

First name: JOHN PAUL

Born: February 15, 1923

Age: 22

Hometown: Pennsylvania, USA

Family: Peter E. Kerlin (father)
Helen (Domjancich) Kerlin (mother)
Mary Kerlin (sister)
Rose Kerlin (sister)
Peter Robert Kerlin (brother)
George S. Kerlin (brother)
Helen Kerlin (sister)

MILITARY SERVICE

Servicenumber: O-1996038

Rank: 2nd Lieutenant — Function: Pilot

Squadron: 513 Fighter Squadron — Group: 406 Fighter Group - 9th Air Force

PLANE DATA

Serial number: 42-28893

Type: Republic P-47D-28-RA Thunderbolt

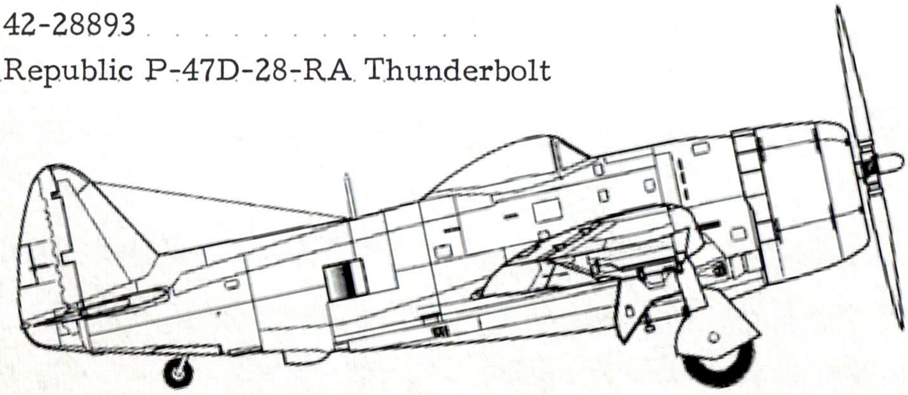

Registration: 4P-V

Nickname:

MACR: 12797

CIRCUMSTANCE OF DECEASE

Date of death: February 28, 1945

Place of death: Kelzenberg, Germany

Cemetery: Mount Olivet Catholic Cemetery, Aliquippa, Beaver County, Pennsylvania, USA

Gravenumber: Section C, Lot 78, Grave 5

Headstone ABMC:

Other information: Shot down in an air battle by Focke-Wulf Fw 190D-9 flown by Oblt. Wilhelm Hofmann of JG 26/5 at Kelzenberg, southeast of Monchengladbach, Germany.

Memory Stone: not available

Photo: find a grave

IDENTIFICATION

Name: DUFFORD
First name: WILLIAM TROY
Born: January 20, 1923
Age: 22
Hometown: Butler County, Pennsylvania, USA

Family: Troy Eugene Dufford (father)
Mollie Irene Louise (Truby) Dufford (mother)
Robert Dufford (brother)
Alona Dufford (sister)

Photo: 366 fighter assosiation

MILITARY SERVICE

Servicenumber: not available
Rank: Flight Officer
Function: Pilot
Squadron: 391 Fighter Squadron
Group: 366 Fighter Group - 9th Air Force

PLANE DATA

Serial number: 42-28665
Type: Republic P-47D-28-RA Thunderbolt

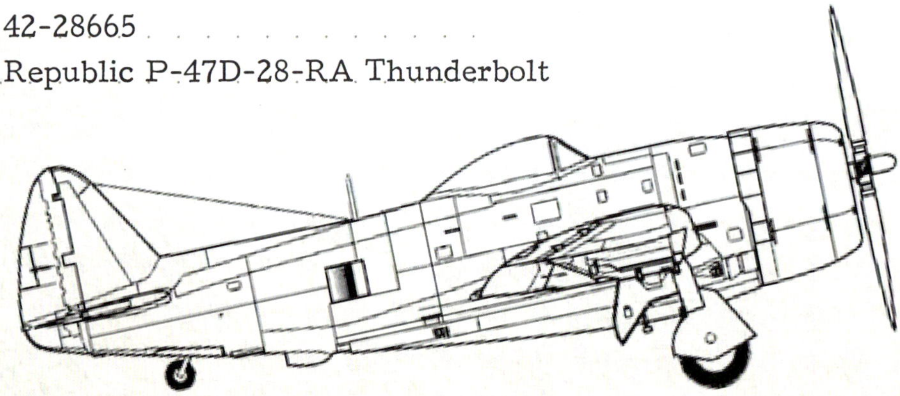

Registration: A8-
Nickname:
MACR: 12955

CIRCUMSTANCE OF DECEASE

Date of death: March 9, 1945

Place of death: Near Wesel, Germany

Cemetery: Arlington National Cemetery, Arlington, Arlington County, Virginia, USA

Gravenumber: Sec: 34, Site: 4364

Headstone ABMC:

Other information: F/O William Dufford was last seen going down with his ship smoking at Wesel after dogfight with enemy aircraft. Shot down by Fw 190D-9 believed flown by Uffz. Fritz Hanusch of JG 26/6 at Wallach near Wesel, Germany.
Returned to USA from The Netherlands American Cemetery and Memorial, The Netherlands. Interred on 24 August 1949.

Memory Stone: WILLIAM T
DUFFORD
PENNSYLVANIA
FLIGHT OFFICER
366 AFF
FIGHTER CP
WORLD WAR II
JANUARY 20 1923
MARCH 9 1945

Photo: find a grave

Photo: find a grave

- - - REGISTRATION FORM - - -

Photo: find a grave

IDENTIFICATION

Name: COBBE
First name: THOMAS DONALD
Born: October 4, 1921
Age: 24
Hometown: Los Angeles County, California, USA

Family: Francis C. Cobbe (father)
Nellie (McKinnon) Cobbe (mother)

MILITARY SERVICE

Servicenumber: O-763496
Rank: 1st Lieutenant | Function: Pilot
Squadron: 391 Fighter Squadron | Group: 366 Fighter Group - 9th Air Force

PLANE DATA

Serial number: 42-26340
Type: Republic P-47D-22 Thunderbolt

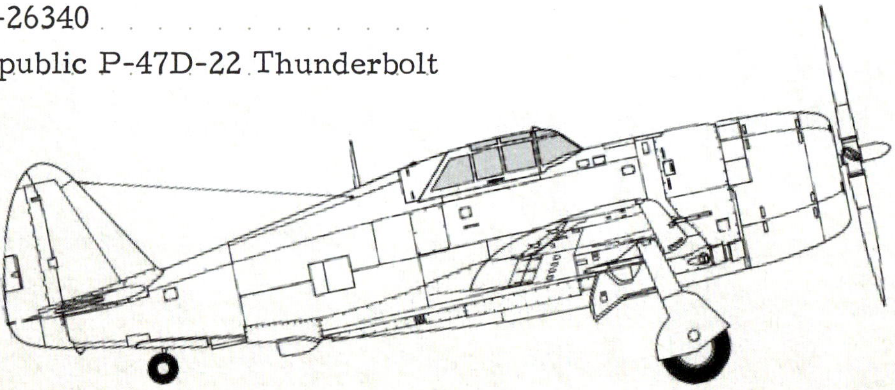

Registration: A8-
Nickname:
MACR: 13106

CIRCUMSTANCE OF DECEASE

Date of death:	March 14, 1945
Place of death:	Königshardt, Germany
Cemetery:	Netherlands American Cemetery and Memorial, The Netherlands
Gravenumber:	Tablets of the Missing
Headstone ABMC:	COBBE THOMAS D 1 LT 391 FTR SQ 366 FTR GP CALIFORNIA
Other information:	The target was a double track rail line at Hüls, Germany, with a locomotive and 20 cars on one track heading west and 30 plus freight cars idle on the other track. Direct hits were observed. 1st Lt Thomas D. Cobbe's plane was hit by flak at 3048 meters (10.000 feet) over Dinslaken and was last seen spinning in on fire. The plane was lost in the haze at 15:35 hours north of Königshardt, Germany. His body was never recovered.

Memory Stone:

Photo: 366 fighter assosiation

IDENTIFICATION

Photo: find a grave

Name:	MAZAL
First name:	PAUL WILLIAM
Born:	November 19, 1922
Age:	22
Hometown:	Loomis, Placer County, California, USA
Family:	John Charles Mazal (father)
	Helen C. Mazal (mother)
	Carl E. Mazal (brother)

MILITARY SERVICE

Servicenumber:	O-763693		
Rank:	1st Lieutenant	Function:	Pilot
Squadron:	513 Fighter Squadron	Group:	406 Fighter Group - 9th Air Force

PLANE DATA

Serial number:	44-33185
Type:	Republic P-47D-30-RA Thunderbolt

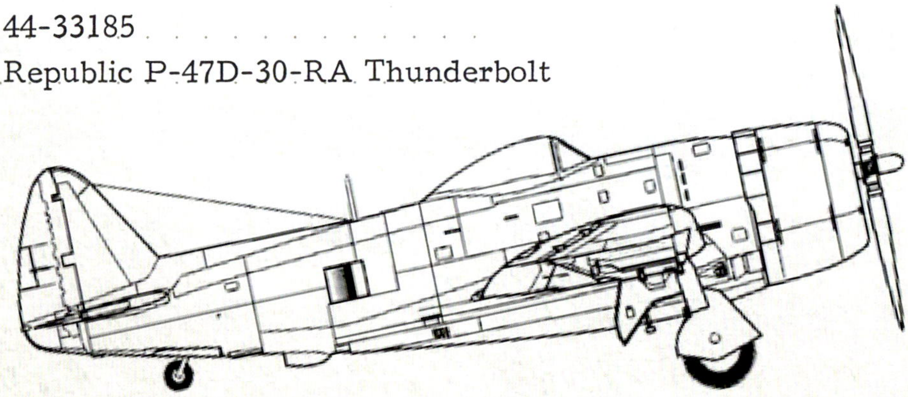

Registration:	4P-
Nickname:	
MACR:	13166

CIRCUMSTANCE OF DECEASE

Date of death: March 19, 1945

Place of death: Werl Buderich, Germany

Cemetery: Henri-Chapelle American Cemetery and Memorial, Belgium

Gravenumber: Tablets of the Missing

Headstone ABMC: MAZAL PAUL W ✻
1 LT 513 FTR SQ 406 FTR GP CALIFORNIA

Other information: The aircraft was hit by flak, cought fire and, crashed in the area of the aerodrome at Werl, Germany. Paul W. Mazal was declared Missing in Action.
The remains of Paul W. Mazal were recovered on May 14, 2007 and identified. Per family tradition, the remains were cremated and spread over the Sierra Highs, California, USA. On the Tablets of the Missing, a rosette has been placed next to his name to indicate that he has been recovered.

Memory Stone:

Photo: find a grave

- - - REGISTRATION FORM - - -

IDENTIFICATION

Photo: find a grave

Name: McVAY
First name: JAMES MORTIMER
Born: 1920
Age: 25
Hometown: Pittsburgh, Pennsylvania, USA

Family: Martha M. McVay (sister)

MILITARY SERVICE

Servicenumber: O-821524
Rank: 2nd Lieutenant
Function: Pilot
Squadron: 514 Fighter Squadron
Group: 406 Fighter Group - 9th Air Force

PLANE DATA

Serial number: 44-33290
Type: Republic P-47D-30-RA Thunderbolt

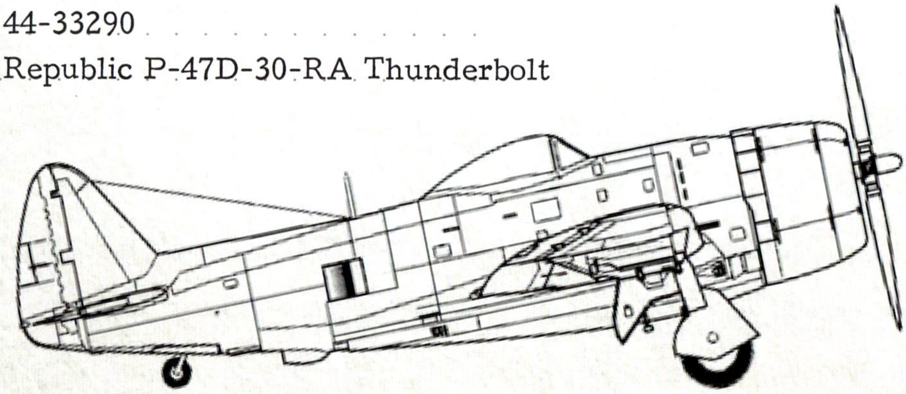

Registration: 07-
Nickname:
MACR: 13221

CIRCUMSTANCE OF DECEASE

Date of death:	March 21, 1945
Place of death:	Haltern am See, Germany
Cemetery:	Ardennes American Cemetery and Memorial, Belgium
Gravenumber:	Plot D, Row 3, Grave 45
Headstone ABMC:	JAMES M. MC VAY 2 LT 514 FTR SQ 406 FTR GP PENNSYLVANIA MAR 21 1945
Other information:	Statement from 1st Lt H.C. Porter: We were flying an armed recce mission in Germany and had completed our bombing and strafing attacks on the enemy and were heading for our base when just Northwest of Haltern, Germany I saw three burst of 88mm flak at 9500. Just at that time Lt Mc Cay called out that he was hit, I then noticed smoke coming from the right side of the engine. I went over to check for fire when Lt Mc Vay dropped off on his right wing, canopy came off and then his ship went over on its back and then headed straight down. I did not see Lt Mc Vay bail out or the plane crash. Time that Lt Mc Vay was hit was at 0927 hours.
Memory Stone:	

--- REGISTRATION FORM ---

IDENTIFICATION

Photo: find a grave

Name: FOWLER

First name: GORDON WADSWORTH

Born: May 18, 1917

Age: 27

Hometown: Newark, New Jersey, USA

Family: Hiram Leo Fowler (father)
Bonnie Mary Wadsworth (mother)
Jean Fowler Fassett (sister)

MILITARY SERVICE

Servicenumber: O-428467

Rank: Major

Function: Pilot

Squadron: 513 Fighter Squadron

Group: 406 Fighter Group - 9th Air Force

PLANE DATA

Serial number: 44-33233

Type: Republic P-47D-30-RA Thunderbolt

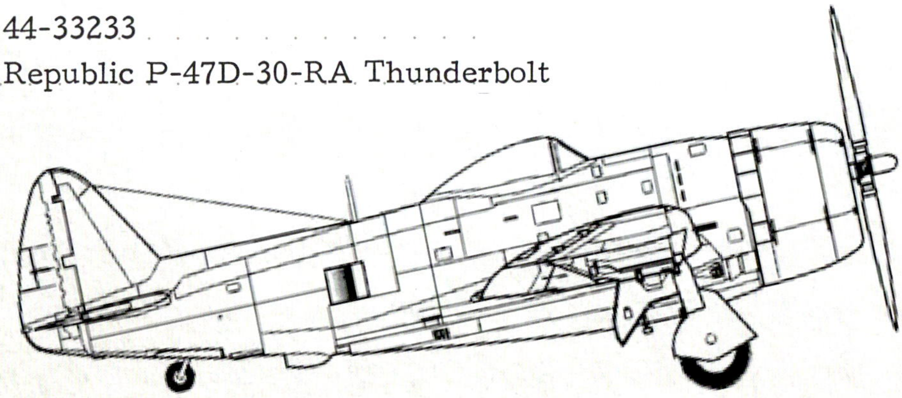

Registration: 4P-

Nickname:

MACR: 13503

CIRCUMSTANCE OF DECEASE

Date of death: March 24, 1945

Place of death: Near Wesel, Germany

Cemetery: Cedar Lawn Cemetery, Paterson, Passaic County, New Jersey, USA

Gravenumber:

Headstone ABMC:

Other information: Killed in action while in support of Allied airborne operation in crossing the Rhine. The plane was hit by flak and crashed NW of Wesel, Germany. Pilot bailed out and killed.
He was initially buried in the Netherlands American Cemetery and Memorial, The Netherlands before being brought home and buried in New Jersey, USA.
There is a Memorial Stone at the Cedar Lawn Cemetery, Paterson, Passaic County, New Jersey, USA.

Memory Stone: IN LOVING MEMORY OF GORDON WADSWORTH FOWLER LT.COL. U.S.A.A.C. BORN MAY 18, 1917 KILLED IN ACTION MARCH 24, 1945 WHILE IN SUPPORT OF ALLIED AIR-BORNE OPERATIONS IN CROSSING THE RHINE NEAR WESSEL, GERMANY. BURRIED IN THE U.S. MILITARY CEMETERY, MARGRATEN, HOLLAND

Photo: find a grave

Photo: find a grave

IDENTIFICATION

Name: SWEET
First name: BERNARD
Born: October 5, 1919
Age: 25
Hometown: Rushford, Allegany County, New York, USA

Family: Laurence A. Sweet (brother)
Madeline Sweet (sister)
Frances Westfall (fiance)

Photo: find a grave

MILITARY SERVICE

Servicenumber: O-811975
Rank: Captain
Function: Pilot
Squadron: 514 Fighter Squadron
Group: 406 Fighter Group - 9th Air Force

PLANE DATA

Serial number: 44-20717
Type: Republic P-47D-30-RE Thunderbolt

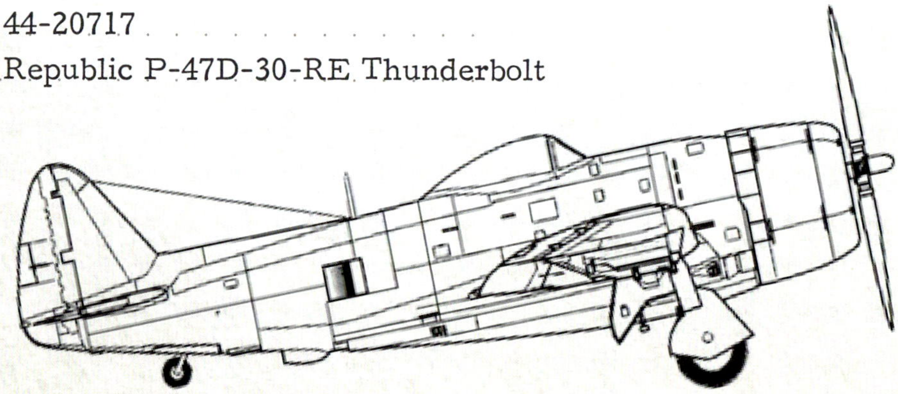

Registration: O7-W
Nickname:
MACR: not available

CIRCUMSTANCE OF DECEASE

Date of death:	March 25, 1945
Place of death:	Y-29 Asch, Belgium
Cemetery:	Netherlands American Cemetery and Memorial, The Netherlands
Gravenumber:	Plot C, Row 15, Grave 18
Headstone ABMC:	BERNARD SWEET CAPT 514 FTR SQ 406 FTR GP NEW YORK MAR 25 1945
Other information:	Crashed landing at Y-29 Asch, possibly colliding with Republic P-47 Thunderbolt 42-28615 taxying at Y-29 Asch. The pilot was killed and the aircraft was destroyed.

Memory Stone:

IDENTIFICATION

Photo: find a grave

Name: STANG
First name: ALAN JOHN
Born: August 30, 1920
Age: 25
Hometown: Illinois, USA

Family: Carolyn R. Perkins (wife)
Albin J. Stang (father)
Mabel Stang (mother)
Thomas A. Stang (brother)
Carol J. Stang (sister)

MILITARY SERVICE

Servicenumber: O-887266
Rank: 1st Lieutenant
Function: Pilot
Squadron: 512 Fighter Squadron
Group: 406 Fighter Group - 9th Air Force

PLANE DATA

Serial number: 44-32948
Type: Republic P-47D-30-RA Thunderbolt

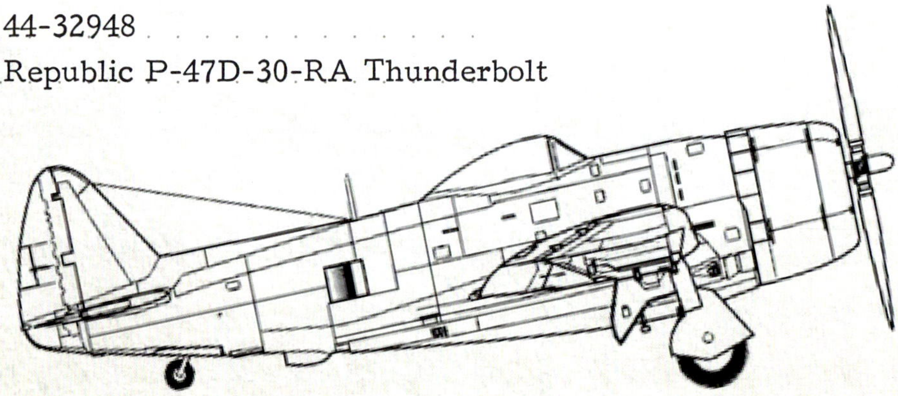

Registration: L3-
Nickname:
MACR: 14457

CIRCUMSTANCE OF DECEASE

Date of death: April 9, 1945

Place of death: Liedenburg, Germany

Cemetery: Mount Emblem Cemetery, Elmhurst, DuPage County, Illinois, USA

Gravenumber:

Headstone ABMC:

Other information: The 512th squadron took off from the Y-29 on close support mission and air recce of the Hannover-Celle area. The plane of 1st Lieutenant Stang was hit by flak, crashed into ground and spun over in flames at Liedenburg, Germany.

Memory Stone: ALAN J. STANG
1ST LT. U.S.ARMY AIR CORPS
1920 1945
KILLED IN ACTION OVER GERMANY

Photo: find a grave

Photo: find a grave

IDENTIFICATION

Photo: find a grave

Name: BOLLE
First name: JOHN ELLEGARDE
Born: 1918
Age: 27
Hometown: Norfolk County, Massachusetts, USA

Family: Helen E. Bolle (wife)
Viggo Bolle (father)
Beatrice A. Bolle (mother)
Aurelia H. Bolle (sister)
Rolf H. Bolle (brother)
Clifton E. Bolle (brother)

MILITARY SERVICE

Servicenumber: O-826370
Rank: 2nd Lieutenant   Function: Pilot
Squadron: 513 Fighter Squadron   Group: 406 Fighter Group - 9th Air Force

PLANE DATA

Serial number: 42-28875
Type: Republic P-47D-28-RA Thunderbolt

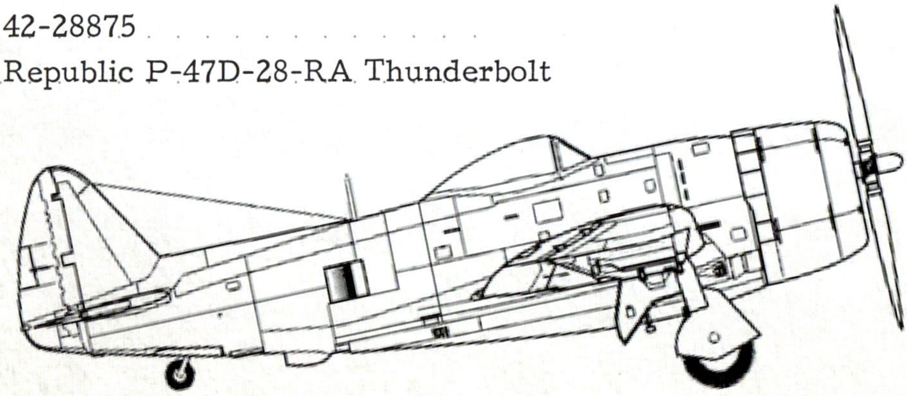

Registration: 4P-F
Nickname:
MACR: 14452

CIRCUMSTANCE OF DECEASE

Date of death: April 12, 1945

Place of death: Magdeburg, Germany

Cemetery: Loraine American Cemetery and Memorial, France

Gravenumber: Plot K, Row 44, Grave 21

Headstone ABMC: JOHN E. BOLLE
2 LT 513 FTR SQ 406 FTR GP
MASSACHUSETTS APR 12 1945

Other information: Shot down by flak and crashed one mile east of Magdeburg, Germany.

Memory Stone:

Photo: Jenne Lantmeeters

Photo: Jenne Lantmeeters

Emblems of the Groups and Squadrons of Y-29 Asch

9th Air Force

366 Fighter Group
(26 November 1944 - 11 April 1945)

389 Fighter Squadron

390 Fighter Squadron

391 Fighter Squadron

8th Air Force

352 Fighter Group
(23 December 1944 - 27 January1945)

428 Fighter Squadron

486 Fighter Squadron

487 Fighter Squadron

9th Air Force

406 Fighter Group
(8 February 1945 - 15 April 1945)

512 Fighter Squadron

513 Fighter Squadron

514 Fighter Squadron

9th Air Force

391 Bomber Group
(16 April 1945 - 27 May 1945)

572 Bomber Squadron

573 Bomber Squadron

574 Bomber Squadron

575 Bomber Squadron

Cemeteries of the Y-29 victims

American Battle Monuments Commission (ABMC)

Source: www.abmc.gov

By the end of World War II, the U.S. Army had established several hundred temporary burial grounds around the world. In 1947 the Secretary of the Army and ABMC selected fourteen sites in foreign countries to become permanent American cemeteries. The chosen locations of these cemeteries corresponded with the course of military operations. They were turned over to ABMC after the interments had been completed by the Graves Registration Service, which was part of the U.S. Army. The configuration of the burials was proposed by an ABMC-appointed cemetery architect and approved by ABMC. After the war all temporary cemeteries not designated as permanent were disestablished by the War Department, and the remains permanently interred in accordance with the directions of the next of kin. In a few instances the next of kin requested that isolated burials be left undisturbed. In these cases, the next of kin assumed responsibility for the care of the grave.

The World War II cemeteries were permanent military burial grounds granted in perpetuity by respective host countries free of charge or taxation. ABMC's World War II cemeteries are closed to further burials, except for the remains of American war dead recovered from time to time in the battle areas.

Headstones

Each grave site for the World War II cemeteries is marked by a headstone of pristine white marble. Headstones of those of the Jewish faith are tapered marble shafts surmounted by a Star of David. Stylized marble Latin crosses mark all others. Annotated on the headstones of the World War II servicemen who could not be identified is: "Here Rests in Honored Glory a Comrade in Arms Known but to God."

Netherlands American Cemetery and Memorial

Successful Allied operations followed landings in Normandy and Southern France. However, logistical shortages slowed momentum. Autumn priority in Northern France, Belgium, and The Netherlands was given to capture of Channel ports and to advance through or around German frontier fortifications (West Wall) into Northern Germany.

Dimensions: 65.5 acres

Headstones: 8,301

Latin crosses: 8,122

Stars of David: 179

Missing in action: 1,722

Sets of brothers: 40

Dedicated: July 7, 1960

Netherlands American Cemetery

Amerikaanse Begraafplaats 1

6269 NA Margraten

The Netherlands

Henri-Chapelle American Cemetery and Memorial

The Henri-Chapelle American Cemetery holds fallen Americans of two major efforts. One involved the First U.S. Army's drive from September through December 1944 through northern France, Belgium, Holland, and Luxembourg into Germany. The second included the Battle of the Bulge and its elimination, enabling allied forces to advance farther into Germany.

Dimensions: 57 acres

Headstones: 7,987

Latin crosses: 7,849

Stars of David: 138

Tablets of the missing: 450

Sets of brothers: 37 sets of two brothers, plus one set of three brothers

Dedicated: July 9, 1960

Henri-Chapelle American Cemetery

157 rue du Memorial Americain

B - 4852 Hombourg

Belgium

Ardennes American Cemetery and Memorial

The Allied main effort in autumn 1944 advanced through Belgium and pushed toward Germany. After sustained winter combat during the Battle of the Bulge, the Allies pursued three major successive objectives: destruction of enemy forces west of the Rhine, seizure of bridgeheads across the river, and then coordinated drives into the heart of Germany.

Dimensions: 90.5 acres

Headstones: 5,311

Latin crosses: 5,183

Stars of David: 128

Tablets of the missing: 462

Sets of brothers: 11

Dedicated: July 11, 1960

Ardennes American Cemetery

Route du Condroz, 164

B-4121 Neuville-en-Condroz

Belgium

Luxembourg American Cemetery and Memorial

Germany launched its last major counteroffensive on December 16, 1944. The attack through the Ardennes had Antwerp as its objective. The assault pierced American lines on a 45-mile front. American soldiers' heroic efforts contained the shoulders of the salient.

Dimensions: 50.5 acres

Headstones: 5,076

Latin crosses: 4,958

Stars of David: 118

Tablets of the missing: 371

Sets of brothers: 22

Dedicated: July 4, 1960

Luxembourg American Cemetery

50, Val du Scheid

L-2517 Luxembourg

Luxembourg

Lorraine American Cemetery and Memorial

Third U.S. Army resumed its pursuit of German forces across eastern France in early September 1944. Seventh U.S. Army, reinforced by the French First Army, advanced northward after landings in southern France. The Ninth Air Force and First Tactical Air Force rendered vital air support throughout the operations.

Dimensions: 113.5 acres

Headstones: 10,487

Latin crosses: 10,285

Stars of David: 202

Missing in action: 444

Sets of brothers: 30

Dedicated: July 19, 196

Lorraine American Cemetery

Avenue de Fayetteville

57500 St. Avold

France

Cambridge American Cemetery and Memorial

After forestalling German invasion in 1940, the United Kingdom became the hub of offensive action against Axis powers in Europe. American reinforcement and presence expanded massively from sea and air. The strategic bombing campaign flown from East Anglia crippled German war power. Allied ground, naval, and air forces set forth from the UK for D-Day 1944, and Germany's ultimate defeat. The Cambridge American Cemetery and Memorial is the only World War II American military cemetery in the United Kingdom.

Dimensions: 30.5

Headstones: 3,812

Latin crosses: 3,731

Stars of David: 81

Tablets of the missing: 5,127

Sets of brothers: 3

Dedicated: July 16, 1956

Cambridge American Cemetery

Madingley Road

Coton Cambridge CB23 7PH

United Kingdom

The Commonwealth War Graves Commission (CWGC)

Source: Wikipedia

The Commonwealth War Graves Commission (CWGC) is an intergovernmental organization of six independent member states whose principal function is to mark, record and maintain the graves and places of commemoration of Commonwealth of Nations military service members who died in the two World Wars. The Commission is also responsible for commemorating Commonwealth civilians who died as a result of enemy action during World War II. The Commission was founded by Sir Fabian Ware and constituted through Royal Charter in 1917 named the Imperial War Graves Commission. The change to the present name took place in 1960.

The Commission, as part of its mandate, is responsible for commemorating all Commonwealth war dead individually and equally. To this end, the war dead are commemorated by name on a headstone, at an identified site of a burial, or on a memorial. War dead are commemorated uniformly and equally, irrespective of military or civil rank, race or creed.

The Commission is currently responsible for the continued commemoration of 1.7 million deceased Commonwealth military service members in 153 countries. Since its inception, the Commission has constructed approximately 2,500 war cemeteries and numerous memorials. The Commission is currently responsible for the care of war dead at over 23,000 separate burial sites and the maintenance of more than 200 memorials worldwide. In addition to commemorating Commonwealth military service members, the Commission maintains, under arrangement with applicable governments, over 40,000 non-Commonwealth war graves and over 25,000 non-war military and civilian graves. The Commission operates through the continued financial support of the member states: United Kingdom, Canada, Australia, New Zealand, India and South Africa.

CWGC

Commonwealth War Graves Commission

BRUSSELS TOWN CEMETERY

Brussels Town Cemetery contains 54 Commonwealth burials of the First World War and a further 587 from the Second World War, 4 of which are unidentified. There are also 35 foreign national burials here and 5 non world war service burials.

CHARLEROI COMMUNAL CEMETERY

The 270 Commonwealth servicemen of the First World War buried in the communal cemetery either died as prisoners of war, or after the Armistice. The cemetery also contains 38 Second World War burials, most of them airmen, and 23 war graves of other nationalities.

LEOPOLDSBURG WAR CEMETERY

There are about 35 original burials in Leopoldsburg War Cemetery associated with isolated engagements in or near the town in May 1940. Of the remainder, some are burials from a military hospital which was established at Leopoldsburg during the latter part of 1944 and others were brought into the cemetery from the surrounding district. There are now 767 Commonwealth burials of the Second World War in the cemetery, 16 of them unidentified, and a number of Polish and Dutch war graves.

VENRAY WAR CEMETERY

The burials in the cemetery date from October 1944 to March 1945. Venray War Cemetery contains 692 Commonwealth burials of the Second World War, 30 of them unidentified, and one Polish burial.

Y-29 Monument / memorial

Y-29 Monument
at the start of the runway

Airfield Y-29

Constructed in 1944 by

The 852nd Engr. Avn. Bn.

Used by:

366th F.G. - 352nd F.G

406th F.G. - 391st B.G.

Zutendaal June 11th 1984

Y-29 Memorial
at the church of Wiemesmeer, Zutendaal

Y-29 ASCH CASUALTIES IN ALPHABETIC ORDER

NAME	FIRST NAME	FIGHTER GROUP	SQUADRON	DATE	CEMETERY	PAGE
Aageberg	James	366	390	January 21, 1945	Henri-Chapelle, B	62
Abbott	Earl	352	328	January 24, 1945	Cambridge, UK	66
Akin	John	406	512	February 25, 1945	Margraten, NL	90
Aldrin	Roger	442TCG	305	November 30, 1944	Henri-Chapelle, B	16
Beverly	Kenneth	366	391	March 13, 1945	Margraten, NL	106
Boehm	Robert	366	389	December 20, 1944	North Dakota, USA	36
Bolle	John	406	513	April 12, 1945	St Avold, F	122
Cobbe	Thomas	366	391	March 14, 1945	Margraten, NL	108
Colbroth	James	366	391	December 19, 1944	Henri-Chapelle, B	34
Cutshall	Edward	366	390	November 26, 1944	Tennessee, USA	10
Davies	William	69	RAF	February 24, 1945	Evere, B	88
Dean	Paul	784	Battery D	March 1, 1945	Tennessee, USA	102
Deja	Henry	406	512	February 20, 1945	Idaho, USA	70
Downs	Edward	366	389	March 1, 1945	Delaware, USA	96
Duffin	Bernard	442TCG	305	November 30, 1944	Henri-Chapelle, B	18
Dufford	William	366	391	March 9, 1945	Arlington, USA	104
Dunton	Wallace	366	390	November 26, 1944	California, USA	12
Earley	Joseph	366	389	January 13, 1945	Luxembourg, L	60
Ford	Alfred	406	512	February 22, 1945	Michigan, USA	74
Fowler	Gordon	406	513	March 24, 1945	New Jersey, USA	114
Gildersleeve	John	406	514	February 20, 1945	Neupré, B	72
Graves	Richard	406	513	February 23, 1945	Neupré, B	80
Hall	Ivan	Roy. Can. Eng.	2Bat.B	December 16, 1944	Leopoldsburg, B	32
Halterman	Claude	366	390	February 28, 1945	Margraten, NL	92
Hass	Floyd	366	391	January 22, 1945	Henri-Chapelle, B	64
Holland	George	406	514	February 22, 1945	Neupré, B	76
Howard	Hugh	352	328	December 31, 1944	Kentucky, USA	56
Johnson	Hilding	366	391	December 25, 1944	Neupré, B	42
Jones	John	366	391	December 24, 1944	New Jersey, USA	38
Kerlin	John	406	513	February 28, 1945	Pennsylvania, USA	94
Leake	Farrer	442TCG	305	November 30, 1944	Henri-Chapelle, B	20
Maloney	Keith	406	512	February 13, 1945	Neupré, B	68
Marshall	William	69	RAF	February 24, 1945	Evere, B	84
Mazal	Paul	406	513	March 19, 1945	Henri-Chapelle, B	110
McCauley	William	366	389	March 1, 1945	Alabama, USA	98
McKinley	Albert	366	391	December 24, 1944	Massachusetts, USA	40
McVay	James	406	514	March 21, 1945	Neupré, B	112
Monaghan	James	69	RAF	February 24, 1945	Evere, B	86
Pease	Stephen	366	389	March 1, 1945	Margraten, NL	100
Peterson	Elmer	366	389	December 27, 1944	California, USA	52
Preddy	George	352	328	December 25, 1944	St Avold, F	44
Preece	Dennis	Royal Engineers		December 26, 1944	Leopoldsburg, B	46
Priddy	Henry	366	391	December 1, 1944	Margraten, NL	28

NAME	FIRST NAME	FIGHTER GROUP	SQUADRON	DATE	CEMETERY	PAGE
Shorey	Frederick	Royal Engineers		December 26, 1944	Charleroi, B	48
Simpson	George	442TCG	305	November 30, 1944	New Jersey, USA	22
Smart	Raymond	366	389	February 23, 1945	Margraten, NL	82
Smith	Philip	366	HQ	November 30, 1944	Pennsylvania, USA	26
Spielman	Morgan	406	514	February 22, 1945	Indiana, USA	78
Stang	Alan	406	512	April 9, 1945	Illinois, USA	120
Steinfeld	Bernard	366	389	December 27, 1944	Luxembourg, L	54
Stryker	Paul	366	391	December 1, 1944	Virginia, USA	30
Sweet	Bernard	406	514	March 25, 1945	Margraten, NL	116
Tafel	Carl	352	487	December 26, 1944	Kentucky, USA	50
Taylor	James	366	389	March 26, 1945	Margraten, NL	118
Webber	Donald	183	RAF	January 1, 1945	Venray, NL	58
Wilson	Arthur	92 BG	327 BS	November 26, 1944	Margraten, NL	14
Wright	Harold	442TCG	305	November 30, 1944	Henri-Chapelle, B	24

Republic P-47D-28-RA Thunderbolt (42-28887) of the 512th Fighter Squadron (L3-G), 406th Fighter Group at Y-29 Asch. This plane was shot down in an aerial combat by a Focke-Wulf FW 190D-9 flown by Lt. Peter Crump of JG 26/13 near Münster, Germany on March 28, 1945. The pilot of the Thunderbolt, Lt. Vern J. Hendershott, parachuted behind enemy lines near Münster and was rescued by rapidly advancing US. Troops.

Photo: Imperial War Museum

Source

Books

352nd Fighter Group Association; The Bluenosed Bastards of Bodney; Fine Books Publishing Company, Charlotte, North Carolina, USA; 2000.

Brandt Steven A.; The 406th Fighter Group in World War II; True History Books, Sabin Court Colorado Springs, USA; 2012.

Brulle Robert V.; Angels Zero, P-47 Close Air Support in Europe; Smithsonian Institution, Washington, USA; 2000.

Keay Danny I.P.; Roscoe Red Three Is Missing, The true story of one of America's Second World War MIA's, 1LT Paul W. Mazal and the men who brought him home; Dog Ear Publishing, Indianapolis, USA; 2012.

Manrho John and Pütz Ron; Bodenplatte, The Luftwaffe's Last Hope; Stackpole Books, Mechanicsburg, Pennsylvania, USA; 2010.

Noah Joe and Sox Samuel L. Jr; George Preddy, Top Mustang Ace; Preddy Memorial Foundation, Greensboro, North Carolina, USA; 1991.

Parker Danny S.; To Win The Winter Sky, Air War over the Ardennes, 1944-1945; Combined Books, Conshocken, Pennsylvania, USA; 1994.

Peterson John and Wozer John T.; The War We Fought, 366th Fighter Group, Hun Hunters, 1943-1946; Fine Books Publishing Company, St. Augustine, Florida, USA; 2007.

Rust Kenn C.; The 9th Air Force in World War II; Aero Publishers, Fallbrook, California, USA; 1970.

Stout Jay A.; Fighter Group, The 352nd "Blue-Nosed Bastards" in World War II; Stackpole Books, Mechanicsburg, Pennsylvania, USA; 2012.

Vzw Heemkring Heidebloemke: Heidebloemke; driemaandelijks tijdschrift, Genk, Belgium.

Republic P-47D-30-RE Thunderbolt (44-20428) of the 514th Fighter Squadron (O7-I), 406th Fighter Group at Y-29 Asch. Nickname: "My Baby".

Photo: Imperial War Museum

Websites

366th Fighter Association
https://www.366fighterassociation.net

Aircrew Remembered:
http://aircrewremembered.com

American Battle Monuments Commission:
https://www.abmc.gov

American Overseas Memorial Day Association
https://www.aomda.org

Commonwealth War Graves Commission:
https://www.cwgc.org

Fields of Honor – Database:
https://www.fieldsofhonor-database.com

Find A Grave:
https://www.findagrave.com

Republic P-47 Thunderbolt database:
http://p-47.database.pagesperso-orange.fr

USASC-USAAS-USAAC-USAAF-USAF Military Aircraft Serials:
http://www.joebaugher.com

406th WWII Fighter Group - boven de website
http://www.406thfightergroup.org

Thanks

Gordt Lantmeeters

Christopher Marshall

Jenne Lantmeeters

Kris Reumers

Luc Meyvis

Lucy Daily

Vera Hermans

Republic P-47D-28-RA Thunderbolt (42-29245) of the 390th Fighter Squadron (B2-B bar), 366th Fighter Group. This plane was shot down by flak near Wesel, Germany March 24, 1945. The pilot bailed out an evaded capture.

Photo: Heemkring Zutendaal

Republic P-47D-30-RA Thunderbolt (44-33211) of the 512th Fighter Squadron (L3-V), 406th Fighter Group. The plane had a mid-air collision on March 10, 1945 with P-47D 44-20561 near Neuss, Germany. The pilot was able to land with his plane. The pilot of the other plane bailed out and survived, but the aircraft was destroyed.

Photo: Heemkring Zutendaal